Richard Holmes

is the author of *Shelley: the Pursuit*, for which he won the Somerset Maugham Prize in 1974, *Footsteps: Adventures of a Romantic Biographer* (1985), described by Michael Holroyd as 'a modern masterpiece', *Dr Johnson & Mr Savage* (1993), which won the 1993 James Tait Black Prize, and *Coleridge: Early Visions*, winner of the 1989 Whitbread Book of the Year Prize. He is a Fellow of the Royal Society of Literature and in 1992 was made an OBE. He lives in London and Norwich, with the novelist Rose Tremain.

SHELLEY ON LOVE

SELECTED WRITINGS

RICHARD HOLMES

Flamingo
An Imprint of HarperCollins*Publishers*

Flamingo
An Imprint of HarperCollins*Publishers*
77–85 Fulham Palace Road,
Hammersmith, London w6 8JB

Published by Flamingo 1996
9 8 7 6 5 4 3 2

First published in Great Britain by
Anvil Press Poetry 1980

Copyright © Richard Holmes 1980

Richard Holmes asserts the moral right to
be identified as the editor of this work

Photograph of Richard Holmes by
Irmeli Jung

ISBN 0 00 655012 6

Set in Linotron Bembo by
Rowland Phototypesetting Ltd
Bury St Edmunds, Suffolk

Printed and bound in Great Britain by
Caledonian International Book Manufacturing Ltd, Glasgow

To Peter and Judy Jay

Wake the serpent not – lest he
Should not know the way to go, –
Let him crawl which yet lies sleeping
Through the deep grass of the meadow!
Not a bee shall hear him creeping,
Not a may-fly shall awaken
From its cradling blue-bell shaken,
Not the starlight as he's sliding
Through the grass with silent gliding.

('Fragment,' 1819)

Contents

Love Lyrics

Postscript

List of Illustrations

Note to the Second Edition

This anthology was originally intended as an exploration of certain themes that haunt my biography, *Shelley: the Pursuit*, and which have remained with me ever since. It is an investigation of the Shelleyan concept of Love, seen especially through the neglected medium of his prose. Fifteen years later it still seems to me that these prose writings, with their extraordinary mixture of passionate autobiography and idealist philosophy, of radical sexual politics and traditional Platonism, provide a lost key to his whole poetic realm, his mysterious house of visions.

I have taken the chance of this second edition to recall for the reader the beauty of that world in so many of Shelley's love lyrics, which have themselves fallen into neglect, owing perhaps to the unfashionable purity of their forms and music.

My new selection from these poems now completes the book, and will I hope expand its scope and deepen the delight in all Shelley's work. He wrote in the last year of his life: 'I think one is always in love with something or other; the error, and I confess it is not easy for spirits cased in flesh and blood to avoid it, consists in seeking in a mortal image the likeness of what is perhaps eternal. . .'

R.H. Norwich, 1995

Preface

THIS ANTHOLOGY brings together for the first time
Shelley's almost unknown prose writings on the subject of
love. Drawn from his notebooks, his essays, his reviews,
his fictional fragments, his translations, and his continuous
stream of private philosophical speculations, it does not
merely give a Romantic poet's view of romantic passion, but
treats of love at large, in all its forms and manifestations:
childhood and parental; adolescent and idealized; heterosexual and homosexual; domestic and poetic; communal and
monogamous; pagan and Christian; earthly and ideal.
It selects three extracts from the lesser-read longer poems,
which serve to crystallize his attitudes to love at three critical
moments in his personal life: from *Alastor* (1816), from *Julian
and Maddalo* (1818), and from his verse autobiography,
Epipsychidion (1821). The entire text of his wonderfully graceful translation of Plato's *Symposium*, which he made at the
age of 26 during his first summer in Italy, is also rescued
from obscurity.

The book is divided biographically into six thematic sections – Childhood, First Love, Second Marriage, Platonic
Harmonies, Italian Discords, and Eternal Image – so that the
reader may follow closely the development of Shelley's views
in response to his experiences. Each section opens with a
short introduction, filling in biographical details, annotating
some of Shelley's possible sources and influences, and briefly
suggesting further lines of consideration. The individual
extracts then follow (with editorial titles supplied in italics
where necessary); and each piece is given its location in
Shelley's work and date of composition in the list of sources
at the end. The book concludes with an outline chronology of
Shelley's life, allowing equal weight to literary and emotional

events. All the illustrations are specifically discussed some-where in the course of the text: statues, people, or places, of special and sometimes heart-breaking significance to Shelley.

I hope the reader may be surprised by the unexpected cool-ness and clarity of Shelley's prose, his powers of argument and concrete description, his fierce intellectual honesty, his occasionally barbed humour, his disarming ability to admit he cannot understand something or express it properly, and above all the obvious intensity of his own experience of love, so much of it unhappy. At a more theoretical level, Shelley's conception of love lies at the heart of his radical views on social justice, political liberty, and poetry itself, and I hope that these connections too will strike the reader with refresh-ing force and directness, even if he disagrees with them, or finds them not so self-evident as Shelley thought in that great age of revolutionary fervour and creative optimism, when Imagination really did seem to be *au pouvoir*. As for Shelley's mischievously critical views of conventional marriage – 'the dreariest and the longest journey' – the reader will simply have to bring his – or her – own experience to bear on the matter.

Shelley's writings on love were composed between the ages of seventeen and thirty. They form an intellectual and emo-tional portrait of a great poet's beliefs and personality developing from adolescence to the threshold of maturity, when they were tragically cut short by a jealous Destiny. But the rest is not silence: these words scattered 'as from an unextinguished hearth, Ashes and sparks' take us back to the deeper appreciation of his major poetry, and forward to the better comprehension of our own hearts.

RICHARD HOLMES
Greenwich, 1979

1

Childhood

Introduction

THIS FIRST SECTION is the most shadowy and enigmatic, consisting of scattered images, dreams, fragments of autobiography, drawn from notebook entries that were never published in Shelley's lifetime. The subject of childhood always pained Shelley, and next to the death of Harriet, it was the thing he found most difficult to discuss or analyse. The reasons for this are apparent. Shelley's memories of his Sussex upbringing, the 'alienated home' and hated schools (Syon House and Eton), were deeply unhappy; while the history of his own children was catastrophic. An unhappy childhood can often be retrieved in the next generation, through successful parenthood, but Shelley was not granted this, and the vision of the beckoning child in the waves which haunted his last weeks at Lerici (as vividly recounted in Edward Williams's journal) may perhaps have symbolized his consciousness of regret and failure. Such feelings inevitably coloured his whole attitude to love, and give his most idealistic statements a peculiar human poignancy. Nothing can be more mistaken than to suppose that Shelley wrote out of ignorance of the cruelties and mundane domestic tragedies of family life. The facts speak for themselves.

The two children of his first marriage to Harriet Westbrook (1811), Ianthe and Charles, were left entirely in the care of their nineteen-year-old mother from 1814 onwards, supported only by a small annuity. After Harriet's suicide in winter 1816, the hapless pair were placed in protective custody by a Chancery Court Order. Though he eventually obtained legal access, there is no evidence that Shelley ever visited either child after the collapse of this first marriage in 1815. Charles died in boyhood; Ianthe married and emigrated to America.

Of the five children born to Shelley's second wife, Mary Godwin, the first was premature and died after one week in London lodgings in 1815. The second, the beloved William or 'Willmouse', died in Rome from dysentery and fever in 1819, aged four. The third, little Clara – named after her tempestuous aunt Claire Clairmont – died in the lobby of a Venetian hotel from teething fever in 1818, aged two. The fifth was lost in a miscarriage which almost killed Mary at Lerici, one month before Shelley's own death in August 1822. Only Shelley's fourth child by Mary, Percy Florence Shelley, born in that city at the time of the composition of the *Ode to the West Wind*, in autumn 1819, survived into adulthood. He lived to marry and inherit the Sussex estates and title that the poet had derided; but Sir Percy had no male offspring and the direct Shelley line died with him.

For Shelley then, parental and childhood love was inescapably associated with images of pain, grief and bitter regret. He wrote very little either directly about his own childhood, or about his own children (though lines on the death of little William are incorporated into *Adonais*); and this silence separates him from one mainstream of Romantic writing as a whole, the passionate recollected childhood worlds of Wordsworth's *Prelude* and Chateaubriand's *Mémoires d'Outre-Tombe*. Instead, the fragments gathered in this section have a dark, elusive, reluctant quality: incidents glanced at uneasily, dreams half-remembered, or works of sculpture that seem to summon up and embody barely suppressed personal emotion. But if this seems a painful or paradoxical way to start an anthology on love, the reader should perhaps recall the passage of Socratic dialogue in the *Symposium* (which may be found in section 4), where Plato suggests that all love begins in need, the absence of what the heart desires: – '"Is not Love, then, the love of that which is not within its reach . . . that which it has not, that which is not itself, that which it wants: such are the things of which there are desire and love?" – "Assuredly."'

The first extract, 'An Early Schoolfriend', besides giving us a rare glimpse of Shelley at his prep school, also contains virtually the only reference to his mother outside his correspondence. She was a handsome but unaffectionate woman (a great rider and breeder of horses), and the fragment suggests memories of misunderstanding and coldness. The passage was first printed by his old Oxford friend Hogg, who says it was written 'not long before Shelley's death' at Lerici. Thus at the very end of his life, he seems to have been turning back to his earliest days, and it is my belief (supported by other verse fragments) that had he lived, Shelley would have embarked on some more openly autobiographical work, taking up where *Epipsychidion* left off, a development frequently observable in poets at about their thirtieth year to heaven. The dark impersonal philosophizing of *The Triumph of Life* (1822) was not the only way open to Shelley after Lerici. The frankness and charm of this passage, combined with its air of cool appraisal, is typical of Shelley's approach to delicate matters: yet he breaks off rather too abruptly.

The three extracts from the 'Notes on Sculptures' vividly suggest how Shelley preferred an objective image (and the classical legend each represented) to mediate between him and childhood or parental feelings. These are not aesthetic or art-catalogue appreciations in any way, but intensely felt evocations of emotion. For Shelley, each sculptural group represents a sort of frozen mime, rather than a study in form and 'plastic' values. He treats them as theatrical *tableaux*, acting out emotions that seem to haunt him with the power of personal memories. The 'Bacchus and Ampelus' takes him back once more to his schooldays, with an ironic glance at forbidden friendships. The 'Laocoön', with its terrible image of crushing coils, seems to touch on some more hidden sense of paternal pain and helplessness, while the suffering of his children seems to overwhelm Shelley: 'we almost seem to hear his shrieks'. The sharp disagreement with Byron (father of Claire's child Allegra) on interpretation of Laocoön's expression is interesting too.

But the most striking of all is certainly the 'Niobe' description. Niobe was the daughter of Tantalus, whose children were slain by Apollo and Artemis in one of those excesses of anger and jealousy which so frequently convulse the Greek legends. The statue has a literal, mimetic poignancy, since the legend says that her maternal grief reduced her to stone. Shelley was drawn to this sculpture more than any other (except perhaps the Roman Hermaphrodite), and I believe that he associated it both with his wife Mary, and at a deeper, more confused level, with his own mother. He wrote in a letter of 1820: 'I spent the winter at Florence, and dedicated every sunny day to the study of the gallery there; the famous Venus, the Minerva, the Apollino – and more than all, the Niobe and her children, are there. No production of sculpture, not even the Apollo, ever produced on me so strong an effect as this Niobe . . .' Shelley's moving observation of this vast carving, such as the tiny detail of the child's hair gathered into a last knot by the mother's hands, show how deeply he entered into the event portrayed.

The remaining two extracts show Shelley consciously and philosophically trying to study experiences in his childhood, and being defeated by the emotions aroused. For the modern reader the work of Jung on dreams and archetypal images may be relevant here to the whole notion of 'reverie', recollection, and symbolically disguised events. The ideal or 'intellectual' philosophy referred to by Shelley also links up with his notion of non-physical love-making discussed in sections 3 and 4. Above all, the extraordinary incident of invading childhood memory narrated – or rather, acted out through Mary's commentary – in the final extract, vividly illustrates Shelley's extreme sensitivity to objects 'connected with human affections'. It also suggests that he was aware of some subtle system of echoes or 'harmonics' in his own mind, which related visual images (a landscape, a sculpture) to dreams and half-suppressed memories, thus carrying him back to his earliest experiences of love.

Altogether, the fragments gathered in this rather mysterious and elusive first section, and the sad events to which they hesitatingly refer, serve to lend this whole anthology on love a certain dark undertone of suffering, which will sound again in subsequent passages.

An early schoolfriend

The nature of Love and Friendship is very little understood, and the distinctions between them ill established. This latter feeling – at least, a profound and sentimental attachment to one of the same sex, wholly divested of the smallest alloy of sensual intermixture – often precedes the former. It is not right to say, merely, that it is exempt from the smallest alloy of sensuality. It rejects with disdain all thoughts but those of an elevated and imaginative character and the process by which the attachment between two persons of different sexes terminates in a sensual union has not yet begun. I remember forming an attachment of this kind at school. I cannot recall to my memory the precise epoch at which this took place; but I imagine it must have been at the age of eleven or twelve.

The object of these sentiments was a boy about my own age, of a character eminently generous, brave, and gentle; and the elements of human feeling seemed to have been from his birth genially compounded within him. There was a delicacy and a simplicity in his manner, inexpressibly attractive. It has never been my fortune to meet with him since my school-days; but either I confound my present recollections with the delusions of past feelings, or he is now a source of honour and utility to every one around him. The tones of his voice were so soft and winning that every word pierced into my heart, and their pathos was so deep that in listening to him the tears often have involuntarily gushed from my eyes. Such was the being for whom I first experienced the sacred sentiments of friendship. I remember in my simplicity writing to my mother a long account of his admirable qualities and my own devoted attachment. I suppose she thought me out of my wits, for she returned no answer to my letter. I remember we used to walk the whole play-hours up and down by some moss-covered palings, pouring out our hearts in youthful talk. We used to speak of the ladies with whom we were in love, and I remember that our usual practice was to confirm each other in the everlasting fidelity, in which we had bound ourselves towards them and towards each other. I recollect thinking my friendship exquisitely beautiful. Every night, when we parted to go to bed, I remember we kissed each other.

Two friends: young Bacchus and Ampelus

. . . The figures are walking as it were with a sauntering and idle pace and talking to each other as they walk, and this is expressed in the motions of their delicate and flowing forms. One arm of Bacchus rests on the shoulder of Ampelus and the other, the fingers being gently curved as with the burning spirit which animates their flexible joints, is gracefully thrown forward corresponding with the advance of the opposite leg. He has sandals and buskins clasped with two serpent heads, and his leg is cinctured with their skins. He is crowned with vine leaves laden with their crude fruit, and the crisp leaves fall as with the inertness of a lithe and faded leaf over his rich and overhanging hair, which gracefully divided on his forehead falls in delicate wreaths upon his neck and breast. Ampelus with a beast skin over his shoulder holds a cup in his right hand, and with his left half embraces the waist of Bacchus. Just as you may have seen (yet how seldom from their dissevering and tyrannical institutions do you see) a younger and an elder boy at school walking in some remote grassy spot of their playground with that tender friendship towards each other which has so much of love. The countenance of Bacchus is sublimely sweet and lovely, taking a shade of gentle and playful tenderness from the arch looks of Ampelus, whose cheerful face turned towards him, expresses the suggestions of some droll and merry device. It has a divine and supernatural beauty as one who walks through the world untouched by its corruptions, its corrupting cares; it looks like one who unconsciously yet with delight confers pleasure and peace. The flowing fulness and roundness of the breast and belly, whose lines fading into each other, are continued with a gentle motion as it were to the utmost extremity of his limbs. Like some fine strain of harmony which flows

round the soul and enfolds it and leaves it in the soft astonishment of a satisfaction, like the pleasure of love with one
whom we most love, which having taken away desire, leaves
pleasure, sweet pleasure . . .

Laocoön: a father defends his children

The subject of the Laocoön is a disagreeable one, but whether we consider the grouping, or the execution, nothing that remains to us of antiquity can surpass it. It consists of a father and his two sons. Byron thinks that Laocoön's anguish is absorbed in that of his children, that a mortal's agony is blending with an immortal's patience. Not so. Intense physical suffering, against which he pleads with an upraised countenance of despair, and appeals with a sense of its injustice, seems the predominant and overwhelming emotion, and yet there is a nobleness in the expression and a majesty that dignifies torture.

We now come to his children. Their features and attitudes indicate the excess of the filial love and devotion that animates them and swallows up all other feelings. In the elder of the two, this is particularly observable. His eyes are fixedly bent on Laocoön – his whole soul is with – is a part of that of his father. His arm extended towards him, not for protection, but from a wish as if instinctively to afford it, absolutely speaks. Nothing can be more exquisite than the contour of his form and face and the moulding of his lips that are half open, as if in the act of – not uttering any unbecoming complaint, or prayer or lamentation, which he is conscious are alike useless – but addressing words of consolatory tenderness to his unfortunate parent. The intensity of his bodily torments is only expressed by the uplifting of his right foot, which he is vainly and impotently attempting to extricate from the grasp of the mighty folds in which it is entangled.

In the younger child, surprise, pain, and grief seem to contend for mastery. He is not yet arrived at an age when his mind has sufficient self-possession, or fixedness of reason, to analyse the calamity that is overwhelming himself and all that is dear to him. He is sick with pain and horror. We almost seem to hear his shrieks. His left hand is on the head of the snake that is burying its fangs in his side, and the vain and fruitless attempt he is making to disengage it increases the effect. Every limb, every muscle, every vein of Laocoön expresses with the fidelity of life the working of the poison and the strained girding round of the inextricable folds, whose tangling sinuosities are too numerous and complicated to be followed. No chisel has ever displayed with such anatomical fidelity and force the projecting muscles of the arm, whose hand clenches the neck of the reptile, almost to strangulation, and the mouth of the enormous asp, and his terrible fangs widely displayed, in a moment to penetrate and meet within its victim's heart, make the spectator of this miracle of sculpture turn away with shuddering and awe, and doubt the reality of what he sees.

Niobe: a mother defends her child

This figure is probably the most consummate personification of loveliness with regard to its countenance as that of the Apollo of the Vatican is with regard to its entire form that remains to us of Greek Antiquity. It is a colossal figure – the size of a work of art rather adds to its beauty, because it allows the spectator the choice of a greater number of points of view in which to catch a greater number of the infinite modes of expression of which any form approaching ideal beauty is necessarily composed – of a mother in the act of sheltering from some divine and inevitable peril, the last, we will imagine, of her surviving children.

The child terrified we may conceive at the strange destruction of all its kindred has fled to its mother and hiding its head in the folds of her robe and casting up one arm as in a passionate appeal for defence from her, where it never before could have been sought in vain, seems in the marble to have scarcely suspended the motion of her terror as though conceived to be yet in the act of arrival. The child is clothed in a thin tunic of delicatest woof, and her hair is gathered on her head into a knot, probably by that mother whose care will never gather it again. Niobe is enveloped in profuse drapery, a portion of which the left hand has gathered up and is in the act of extending it over the child in the instinct of defending her from what reason knows to be inevitable. The right – as the restorer of it has rightly comprehended – is gathering up her child to her and with a like instinctive gesture is encouraging by its gentle pressure the child to believe that it can give security. The countenance which is the consummation of feminine majesty and loveliness, beyond which the imagination scarcely doubts that it can conceive anything, that master-piece of the poetic harmony of marble, expresses other feelings. There is embodied a sense of the inevitable and rapid destiny which is consummating around her as if it were already over. It seems as if despair and beauty had combined and produced nothing but the sublime loveliness of grief. As the motions of the form expressed the instinctive sense of the possibility of protecting the child and the accustomed and affectionate assurance that she would find protection within her arms, so reason and imagination speak in the countenance the certainty that no mortal defence is of avail.

There is no terror in the countenance – only grief – deep grief. There is no anger – of what avail is indignation against what is known to be omnipotent? There is no selfish shrinking from personal pain; there is no panic at supernatural agency – there is no adverting to herself as herself – the calamity is mightier than to leave scope for such emotion.

Every thing is swallowed up in sorrow. Her countenance in assured expectation of the arrow piercing its victim in her embrace is fixed on her omnipotent enemy. The pathetic beauty of the mere expression of her tender and serene despair, which is yet so profound and so incapable of being ever worn away, is beyond any effect of sculpture. As soon as the arrow shall have pierced her last child, the fable that she was dissolved into a fountain of tears will be but a feeble emblem of the sadness of despair, in which the years of her remaining life, we feel, must flow away . . .

Childhood reveries and idealism

. . . Let us recollect our sensations as children. What a distinct and intense apprehension had we of the world and of ourselves! Many of the circumstances of social life were then important to us which are now no longer so. But that is not the point of comparison on which I mean to insist. We less habitually distinguished all that we saw and felt, from ourselves. They seemed, as it were, to constitute one mass. There are some persons who in this respect are always children. Those who are subject to the state called reverie feel as if their nature were dissolved into the surrounding universe, or as if the surrounding universe were absorbed into their being. They are conscious of no distinction. And these are states which precede, or accompany, or follow an unusually intense and vivid apprehension of life. As men grow up this power commonly decays, and they become mechanical and habitual agents. Thus feelings and then reasonings are the combined result of a multitude of entangled thoughts and of a series of what are called impressions, planted by reiteration.

The view of life presented by the most refined deductions of the intellectual philosophy is that of unity. Nothing exists but as it is perceived. The difference is merely nominal between those two classes of thought which are vulgarly distinguished by the names of ideas and of external objects. Pursuing the same thread of reasoning, the existence of distinct individual minds, similar to that which is employed in now questioning its own nature, is likewise found to be a delusion. The words *I, you, they* are not signs of any actual difference subsisting between the assemblage of thoughts thus indicated, but are merely marks employed to denote the different modifications of the one mind.

Let it not be supposed that this doctrine conducts to the

monstrous presumption that I, the person who now write and think, am that one mind. I am but a portion of it. The words *I* and *you* and *they* are grammatical devices invented simply for arrangement, and totally devoid of the intense and exclusive sense usually attached to them. It is difficult to find terms adequate to express so subtle a conception as that to which the Intellectual Philosophy has conducted us. We are on that verge where words abandon us, and what wonder if we grow dizzy to look down the dark abyss of how little we know . . .

A dream of love recalled

Let us reflect on our infancy, and give as faithfully as possible a relation of the events of sleep . . . I distinctly remember dreaming three several times, between intervals of two or more years, the same precise dream. It was not so much what is ordinarily called a dream; the single image, unconnected with all other images, of a youth who was educated at the same school with myself, presented itself in sleep. Even now, after the lapse of many years, I can never hear the name of this youth, without the three places where I dreamed of him presenting themselves distinctly to my mind.

In dreams, images acquire associations peculiar to dreaming; so that the idea of a particular house, when it recurs a second time in dreams, will have relation with the idea of the same house, in the first time, of a nature entirely different from that which the house excites, when seen or thought of in relation to waking ideas.

I have beheld scenes, with the intimate and unaccountable connection of which with the obscure parts of my own nature, I have been irresistibly impressed. I have beheld a scene which has produced no unusual effect on my thoughts. After the lapse of many years I have dreamed of this scene. It has hung on my memory; it has haunted my thoughts at intervals with the pertinacity of an object connected with human affections. I have visited this scene again. Neither the dream could be dissociated from the landscape, nor the landscape from the dream, nor feelings, such as neither singly could have awakened, from both. But the most remarkable event of this nature which ever occurred to me happened five years ago at Oxford.

I was walking with a friend in the neighbourhood of that city engaged in earnest and interesting conversation. We suddenly turned the corner of a lane, and the view which its high banks and hedges had concealed presented itself. The view consisted of a windmill, standing in one among many plashy meadows, inclosed with stone walls; the irregular and broken ground between the wall and the road on which we stood; a long low hill behind the windmill, and a grey covering of uniform cloud spread over the evening sky. It was that season when the last leaf had just fallen from the scant and stunted ash. The scene surely was a common scene; the season and the hour little calculated to kindle lawless thought; it was a tame uninteresting assemblage of objects, such as would drive the imagination for refuge in serious and sober talk, to the evening fireside and the dessert of winter fruits and wine. The effect which it produced on me was not such as could have been expected. I suddenly remembered to have seen that exact scene in some dream of long – *Here I was obliged to leave off, overcome by thrilling horror.*

NOTE BY MARY SHELLEY This remark closes this fragment, which was written in 1815. I remember well his coming to me from writing it, pale and agitated, to seek refuge in conversation from the fearful emotions it excited. No man, as these fragments prove, had such keen sensations as Shelley. His nervous temperament was wound up by the delicacy of his health to an intense degree of sensibility, and while his active mind pondered for ever upon, and drew conclusions from his sensations, his reveries increased their vivacity, till they mingled with, and made one with thought, and both became absorbing and tumultuous, even to physical pain.

2

First Love

Introduction

LIKE MANY HIGHLY GIFTED young intellectuals, Shelley
was dogmatic rather than affectionate, and began life by
sacrificing his girls to his principles. Nevertheless his
principles – of free love and communal endeavour – are
remarkable, and this section consists largely of theoretical
rather than amorous declarations. Had he been less excep-
tional, and less energetic, he would have remained an
undergraduate at Oxford until 1813, read his prescribed
classical texts, sowed his wild oats, and written nothing of
interest. Instead he became something recognizably modern:
a student without a University, travelling restlessly, involved in political activity (in Wales, in Ireland, in Devon),
reading radical authors (Voltaire, Condorcet, Volney,
Paine, Godwin, Wollstonecraft), and getting intensely
involved with an ever-shifting ménage or commune of
young people from different class-backgrounds, who became
somewhat indiscriminately soul-mates, mistresses, wives,
blood-brothers, muses, co-authors, and confidantes. These
were, after all, the 'times that tried men's souls', and the age
demanded no less: Coleridge and Southey had experimented
with Pantisocracy, and Wordsworth with the French Revolution and Annette Vallon. Shelley was only outstanding for
the fearlessness with which he publicly stated his views (in
poems, in pamphlets, in political meetings), and the impetu-
osity with which he acted upon them. His views on love
were no exception.

The hectic events of the three years covered in this section,
1811–14, may be glimpsed in the Chronology. Suffice it to
recall that Shelley was only eighteen when he eloped with
Harriet Westbrook (then sixteen), and twenty-one when he
eloped with Mary Godwin (then seventeen): the explosive

emotional development between the two is extremely marked, even in the young radical theoretician. To begin with Shelley is typically bookish, and scornful in his attitudes: passionately sincere, arrogant, self-contradictory, and adopting the egalitarian position with all the assurance of a private income. Love is largely an intellectual concept, one dialectical counter in the overall radical position. Nevertheless, he presents the position rather strikingly, with a poetic force. He is anti-Government, anti-Religion, and anti-Matrimony; even if he has private reservations, he argues for Republicanism, Atheism, and a particular form of Free Love. At the same time, emotionally, he is far more puritan than libertine: he believes in strict vegetarianism, dislikes alcohol, rises early, reads voraciously, and makes frequently dismissive references to the physical aspects of love. He is shut in on himself, wounded by rejection from home and University, unable to give emotionally, except perhaps to his friend Hogg. Poor Harriet cannot change much of this, though she bears his first two children, and dreams of a communal farm in Wales (*plus ça change*). It is only Mary Godwin – and also her step-sister Claire – who release the sensual and tender qualities in him during that second elopement: love then becomes a reality, is made flesh, and even the rhythms of his prose are transformed.

Yet who *was* Shelley's first love? The sentimentalist might say Harriet still, or even that early Harriet – Harriet Grove – his schoolboy flame, who received so many letters attacking Christianity. The psychologist might suggest Hogg, his passionate confidante and would-be wife-sharer until 1815. The critic, sensing the sudden enrichment and expansion of his poetry after 1814, might point confidently to Mary: ignoring the fact that Mary brought Claire, too, permanently into his life. Shelley himself was fond of quoting St Augustine's formula at this period of his life: 'Nondum amabam, et amare amabam, quaerebam quid amarem, amans amare . . .' – 'I was not yet in love, and I was in love with the idea of loving; so I sought for something that I might love, since I loved to love . . .' But the biographer, taking all these cues, might answer I think with another question: when did Shelley first understand what love was? And the answer to that certainly takes us as far as *Epipsychidion*.

One point in Shelley's doctrinaire views does not change at this time, and indeed never really changes subsequently: he does not approve of the conventional monogamous marriage. Or rather, he does not think it a very important method of social organization. As he wrote to Hogg in November 1811: 'I attach little value to the monopoly of exclusive cohabitation. You know that I frequently have spoken slightly of it.' It is impossible to understand the later complications of his emotional life without appreciating this. At the same time, Shelley was perhaps more dependent on a closely-knit domestic ménage than most men, and it is ironic to reflect that he was the most married of all the Romantic poets.

Shelley in fact married Harriet *twice*: once in Edinburgh when they eloped in 1811; and again in London in 1814, shortly before he eloped with Mary and Claire to Paris. He also married Mary within three weeks of Harriet's suicide in December 1816, the ceremony being attended by his father-in-law William Godwin, another convinced anti-matrimonialist. (Shelley's daring elopements actually had rather a venerable family tradition behind them: his grandfather, the first baronet, old eccentric Sir Bysshe Shelley who had tried his fortune in America, also succeeded in eloping on two occasions – though he chose county heiresses.) Yet all these marriages were essentially matters of form with Shelley: at first to protect the women in his household, and later to protect the children. The households themselves remained wildly unconventional by the standards of the day, centres of high spirits and constant drama, with money, books, rooms and affection freely shared, and Shelley's newest scheme generating unflagging excitement. To be in love, for the young Shelley, was to be both physically and intellectually on the move: ceaselessly travelling, enquiring, questioning, pursuing the radiant heart's desire.

On the matter of physical sex itself, we are easily led to jump to the obvious conclusion, especially after the revelations of Bloomsbury, and our own experience of the Sixties.

But we can never be quite sure about the sexual manners of Regency England, whether conventional or otherwise. Certainly they were not Victorian; but equally, they were not Californian. One has the impression of both a frankness, and a restrained delicacy of approach, that may be lost to our own knowing, statistical age. When Shelley bathed naked in the mountain streams of the Jura during his second elopement, Mary (with whom he was sleeping) was too modest to join him; Claire, a buxom virginal sixteen, was not. And when, on the same trip, the rats in a seedy tavern-house bedroom frightened Claire with their scamperings, Shelley firmly put her into bed with him and Mary. I suspect that many members of the Shelley circle spent intimate nights together, talking in each others' arms on the couch, or curled up together in front of the fire (Shelley's favourite spot) – and *honi soit qui mal y pense.* But I also suspect that Shelley did at one time have 'Godwinian' schemes for his friend Hogg to share both Harriet and Mary with him, sexually; and that from 1814 onwards, Claire Clairmont at least provided the element of dark, unstable, tempestuous affection that his calm union with Mary required to keep it alive; and that this 'shadow' love occasionally – at moments of crisis – achieved violent sexual expression. But the young radical and lover of this section understands his arguments better, as yet, than his own temperament.

The first extract gives the celebrated essay on free love, which Shelley appended as the ninth Note to his long ideological poem *Queen Mab*, and which later was widely circulated among Chartists and early free-thinking socialists, including the young Frederick Engels. The poem was published in 1813, but the essay belongs to notebook material written some time between 1811–12. It vividly reflects the influence of Shelley's intense and studious reading at this period, and also sadly prophesies the approaching collapse of his marriage to Harriet. The scornful, rapid, but rather rhetorical brilliance of the style is typical of Shelley's early polemic prose. He repeats, sometimes phrase for phrase, his textbooks of the time. In particular he draws on passages from William Godwin's *Political Justice* (the most radical first edition of 1793); Mary Wollstonecraft's *Vindication of the Rights of Woman* (1792); and the Scottish sceptic David Hume's *Essay on Polygamy and Divorce* (1748). In fact Shelley was surprisingly attracted by the Commonsense School of the Edinburgh philosophers, whom he probably heard lecture there in 1811, and again in 1814. Shelley makes admiring references much later in his work to Dugald Stewart and Sir William Drummond, who also – most appropriately – made a study of volcanoes. Yet the fire and urgency of the essay is unmistakably Shelley's. Moreover, beneath the youthful polemic, he is groping towards a new freedom and equality in domestic relationships, a genuine conception of mutual self-discovery and enrichment, far beyond the legalistic idea of 'easy divorce'. Shelley foresees a certain kind of spiritual independence within partnership which is perhaps easier for us to understand today (though not much easier to achieve), with the impact of the Feminist movement, than it was for his outraged contemporaries. The first people to interpret him in this way were probably the post-Victorian writers and reformers of 'advanced' sexual views, such as Edward Carpenter, George Bernard Shaw and the Fabians, and Havelock Ellis – the literary critic turned sexologist. But it is also easy for us to read too much in, anachronistically. Biography reminds us how inexperienced Shelley still was; and it is only possible to read his remarks about children with sad irony.

The essay also reflects the influence of a curious and forgotten novel of the day, *The Empire of the Nairs* (1811) by James Lawrence. It is a three-decker romance based on travellers' accounts of a flourishing matriarchal tribe living in Malabar, on the west coast of India, and is a distant forerunner of those many anthropological studies of kinship patterns which have so affected modern sociology. It contains a Preface advocating free love, co-education, and nude bathing. Regarded as a scandalous text, it was first published in German, and then in French, and greatly intrigued the German Romantic poet and dramatist Friedrich Schiller. Lawrence was another ex-Etonian poet and adventurer, though of dubious reputation, who lived a largely expatriate life in the floating society of several European cities, and eventually acquired or awarded himself the title of Chevalier. He also published a narrative poem, *Love: an Allegory*, describing marriage as a jail; and an early satirical poem *The Bosom Friend* (1791), in praise of the unmentionable upper corset, which Shelley perhaps did not read. At any rate, Shelley's earnest but amused greeting to his fellow campaigner, making reference to both the first two works, is given in the second extract as a curiosity.

Something of what Shelley hoped to put in place of conventional marriage can be glimpsed in the first chapter of his own unfinished historical novel, *The Assassins*, which forms the next extract. He wrote this after the separation from Harriet, and during his hastily improvised travels through France and Switzerland with Mary and Claire in 1814. The rambling, dreamy text reflects the conditions under which it was composed; and the outcast group of idealists 'pitching their tents' in the lost valleys of Lebanon is a projection of their own wanderings. The story, such as it is, takes its inspiration from a fragment of the early Christian or Gnostic legends, concerning an 'obscure community of speculators' who fled into the wilderness after the fall of Jerusalem, carrying with them the uncorrupted principles of primitive communal Christianity. It is the first of Shelley's many evocations of an enlightened community of friends who retire from the false values of modern society, submit themselves to Nature and Reason, and try to share on equal terms love, labour and the pursuit of happiness. 'No longer would the poison of a diseased civilization embrue their very nutriments with pestilence. They would no longer owe their very existence to the vices, the fears, and the follies of mankind. Love, friendship, and philanthropy would now be the characteristic disposers of their industry. It is for his mistress or his friend that the labourer consecrates his toil . . .' In a later section we will see Shelley also questioning the validity of such a 'retirement' from society, as a form of moral escapism; but in the second chapter of the novel he interestingly concludes that such an idealist forced to return to society would inevitably adopt the values of a political terrorist – *viz*. a real 'assassin'.

The extract shows the exotic influence of Rousseau, whom Shelley was beginning to read at this time, and combines rationalism with strong overtones of Nature mysticism. In this Shelley joins a long tradition of communal utopias, which may be traced from Gerrard Winstanley and the seventeenth-century Diggers, via Pantisocracy and numerous American immigrant communities, right through to the wave of communal experiments in Scandinavia, Germany, England and America in the 1960s, and no doubt beyond. It is also particularly interesting for the importance Shelley attaches to the inspiration of primitive Christianity, at a time when he was generally considered to be rabidly anti-religious, quoting and misquoting freely from the New Testament. At a more literary level, his ornate but strangely haunting description of Nature run wild in the valley of Bethzatanai echoes the picture of the Happy Valley in Dr Johnson's *Rasselas* (1759), and foreshadows many subsequent magical retreats in his later poetry – notably the blossoming ruins of the Baths of Cara-calla in *Prometheus Unbound*, and his imaginary 'island of the Sporades' in *Epipsychidion*: all cradles of redeemed love.

The final extract gives the most revealing of a series of letters concerning his separation from Harriet. Addressed – significantly enough – to Hogg, it looks back retrospectively over the emotional upheavals of summer 1814, and gives the most extraordinarily frank and impassioned account of his revulsion from Harriet and his infatuation with Mary. Angry, bitter, ecstatic, self-righteous, pathetically confiding by turns, it shows the unmistakable emergence of the new, explosively loving and tender side of Shelley's nature – 'not a dis-embodied spirit can have undergone a stranger revolution!' At the same time it contains an unhappy and ill-omened omis-sion: there is not a word of the hostages of this love, his children. For two were now waiting to be born – one Har-riet's, and one Mary's.

Against legal marriage

Not even the intercourse of the sexes is exempt from the despotism of positive institution. Law pretends even to govern the indisciplinable wanderings of passion, to put fetters on the clearest deductions of reason, and by appeals to the will, to subdue the involuntary affections of our nature. Love is inevitably consequent upon the perception of loveliness. Love withers under constraint; its very essence is liberty; it is compatible neither with obedience, jealousy, nor fear; it is there most pure, perfect, and unlimited, where its votaries live in confidence, equality, and unreserve.

How long then ought the sexual connection to last? What law ought to specify the extent of the grievances which should limit its duration? A husband and wife ought to continue so long united as they love each other; any law which should bind them to cohabitation for one moment after the decay of their affection would be a most intolerable tyranny, and the most unworthy of toleration. How odious an usurpation of the right of private judgement should that law be considered which should make the ties of friendship indissoluble, in spite of the caprices, the inconsistency, the fallibility, and capacity for improvement of the human mind. And by so much would the fetters of love be heavier and more unendurable than those of friendship, as love is more vehement and capricious, more dependent on those delicate peculiarities of imagination, and less capable of reduction to the ostensible merits of the object.

The state of society in which we exist is a mixture of feudal savageness and imperfect civilization. The narrow and unenlightened morality of the Christian religion is an aggravation of these evils. It is not even until lately that mankind have admitted that happiness is the sole end of the science of ethics, as of all other sciences; and that the fanatical idea of mortifying the flesh for the love of God has been discarded. I have heard, indeed, an ignorant collegian adduce in favour of Christianity its hostility to every worldly feeling!*

But if happiness be the object of morality, of all human unions and disunions; if the worthiness of every action is to be estimated by the quantity of pleasurable sensation it is calculated to produce, then the connection of the sexes is so long sacred as it contributes to the comfort of the parties, and is naturally dissolved when its evils are greater than its benefits. There is nothing immoral in this separation. Constancy has nothing virtuous in itself, independently of the pleasure it confers, and partakes of the temporizing spirit of vice in proportion as it endures tamely moral defects of magnitude in the object of its indiscreet choice. Love is free; to promise for ever to love the same woman is not less absurd than to promise to believe the same creed; such a vow in both cases excludes us from all enquiry. The language of the votarist is this: the woman I now love may be infinitely inferior to many others; the creed I now profess may be a mass of errors and absurdities; but I exclude myself from all future information as to the amiability of the one and the truth of the other, resolving blindly and in spite of conviction to adhere to them: Is this the language of delicacy and reason? Is love of such a frigid heart of more worth than its belief?

The present system of constraint does no more in the majority of instances than make hypocrites or open enemies. Persons of delicacy and virtue, unhappily united to one whom they find it impossible to love, spend the loveliest season of their life in unproductive efforts to appear otherwise than

* The first Christian emperor made a law by which seduction was punished with death; if the female pleaded her own consent, she also was punished with death; if the parents endeavoured to screen the criminals, they were banished and their estates were confiscated; the slaves who might be accessory were burned alive, or forced to swallow melted lead. The very offspring of an illegal love were involved in the consequences of the sentence. Gibbon's *Decline and Fall*, etc., vol. ii, p. 210. See also, for the hatred of the primitive Christians toward love and even marriage, p. 269. [*Shelley's note*]

they are, for the sake of the feelings of their partner or the welfare of their mutual offspring; those of less generosity and refinement openly avoid their disappointment, and linger out the remnant of that union, which only death can dissolve, in a state of incurable bickering and hostility. The early education of their children takes its colour from the squabbles of the parents; they are nursed in a systematic school of ill-humour, violence, and falsehood. Had they been suffered to part at the moment when indifference rendered their union irksome, they would have been spared many years of misery; they would have connected themselves more suitably, and would have found that happiness in the society of more congenial partners, which is for ever denied them by the despotism of marriage. They would have been separately useful and happy members of society, who, while united, were miserable and rendered misanthropical by misery. The conviction that wedlock is indissoluble holds out the strongest of all temptations to the perverse; they indulge without restraint in acrimony and all the little tyrannies of domestic life, when they know that their victim is without appeal. If this connection were put on a rational basis, each would be assured that habitual ill-temper would terminate in separation and would check this vicious and dangerous propensity.

Prostitution is the legitimate offspring of marriage and its accompanying errors. Women, for no other crime than having followed the dictates of a natural appetite, are driven with fury from the comforts and sympathies of society. It is less venial than murder; and the punishment which is inflicted on her who destroys her child to escape reproach is lighter than the life of agony and disease to which the prostitute is irrecoverably doomed. Has a woman obeyed the impulse of unerring nature, society declares war against her, pitiless and eternal war; she must be the tame slave; she must make no reprisals; theirs is the right of persecution, hers the duty of endurance. She lives a life of infamy; the loud and bitter laugh of scorn scares her from all return. She dies of long and lingering disease; yet *she* is in fault; *she* is the criminal; *she* is the froward and untamable child; and society, forsooth, the pure and virtuous matron, who casts her as an abortion from her undefiled bosom! Society avenges herself on the criminals of her own creation; she is employed in anathematizing the vice today, which yesterday she was the most zealous to teach. Thus is formed one-tenth of the population of London; meanwhile the evil is twofold. Young men, excluded by the fanatical idea of chastity from the society of modest and accomplished women, associate with these vicious and miserable beings, destroying thereby all those exquisite and delicate sensibilities whose existence cold-hearted worldlings have denied, annihilating all genuine passion, and debasing that to a selfish feeling which is the excess of generosity and devotedness. Their body and mind alike crumble into a hideous wreck of humanity; idiocy and disease become perpetuated in their miserable offspring, and distant generations suffer for the bigoted morality of their forefathers. Chastity is a monkish and evangelical superstition, a greater foe to natural temperance even than unintellectual sensuality; it strikes at the root of all domestic happiness, and consigns more than half of the human race to misery that some few may monopolize according to law. A system could not well have been devised more studiously hostile to human happiness than marriage.

I conceive that from the abolition of marriage the fit and natural arrangement of sexual connection would result. I by no means assert that the intercourse would be promiscuous; on the contrary, it appears, from the relation of parent to child that this union is generally of long duration and marked above all others with generosity and self-devotion. But this is a subject which it is perhaps premature to discuss. That which will result from the abolition of marriage will be natural and right, because choice and change will be exempted from restraint.

In fact, religion and morality, as they now stand, compose a practical code of misery and servitude; the genius of human happiness must tear every leaf from the accursed book of God ere man can read the inscription on his heart. How would morality, dressed up in stiff stays and finery, start from her own disgusting image should she look in the mirror of nature!

To a fellow-campaigner against marriage, Sir James Lawrence

Lynmouth, Barnstaple, Devon,
August 17, 1812.

Sir,

I feel peculiar satisfaction in seizing the opportunity which your politeness places in my power, of expressing to you personally (as I may say) a high acknowledgement of my sense of your talents and principles, which, before I conceived it possible that I should ever know you, I sincerely entertained. Your 'Empire of the Nairs,' which I read this Spring, succeeded in making me a perfect convert to its doctrines. I then retained no doubts of the evils of marriage – Mrs Wollstonecraft reasons too well for that; but I had been dull enough not to perceive the greatest argument against it, until developed in the 'Nairs,' viz., prostitution both *legal* and *illegal*.

I am a young man, not yet of age, and have now been married a year to a woman younger than myself. Love seems inclined to stay in the prison, and my only reason for putting him in chains, whilst convinced of the unholiness of the act, was, a knowledge that in the present state of society, if love is not thus villainously treated, she, who is most loved, will be treated worse by a misjudging world. In short, seduction, which term could have no meaning, in a rational society, has now a most tremendous one; the fictitious merit attached to chastity has made that a forerunner of the most terrible of ruins, which, in Malabar, would be a pledge of honour and homage. If there is any enormous and desolating crime, of which I should shudder to be accused, it is seduction. – I need not say how much I admire '*Love*'; and little as a British public seems to appreciate its merit, in never permitting it to emerge from a first edition, it is with satisfaction I find, that justice has conceded abroad what bigotry has denied at home.

I shall take the liberty of sending you any little publication I may give to the world. Mrs S. joins with myself in hoping, if we come to London this winter, we may be favoured with the personal friendship of one whose writings we have learnt to esteem.

Yours very truly,
Percy Bysshe Shelley.

An ideal commune

The Assassins: A Romance

CHAPTER I

Jerusalem, goaded on to resistance by the incessant usurp-
ations and insolence of Rome, leagued together its discordant
factions to rebel against the common enemy and tyrant.
Inferior to their foe in all but the unconquerable hope of liberty,
they surrounded their city with fortifications of uncommon
strength, and placed in array before the temple a band
rendered desperate by patriotism and religion. Even the
women preferred to die rather than survive the ruin of their
country. When the Roman army approached the walls of the
sacred city, its preparations, its discipline, and its numbers
evinced the conviction of its leader, that he had no common
barbarians to subdue. At the approach of the Roman army,
the strangers withdrew from the city.

Among the multitudes which from every nation of the
East had assembled at Jerusalem was a little congregation of
Christians. They were remarkable neither for their numbers
nor their importance. They contained among them neither
philosophers nor poets. Acknowledging no laws but those
of God, they modelled their conduct towards their fellowmen by the conclusions of their individual judgement on the
practical application of these laws. And it was apparent from
the simplicity and severity of their manners that this contempt
for human institutions had produced among them a character
superior in singleness and sincere self-apprehension to the
slavery of pagan customs and the gross delusions of anti-
quated superstition. Many of their opinions considerably
resembled those of the sect afterwards known by the name

of Gnostics. They esteemed the human understanding to be the paramount rule of human conduct; they maintained that the obscurest religious truth required for its complete elucidation no more than the strenuous application of the energies of mind. It appeared impossible to them that any doctrine could be subversive of social happiness which is not capable of being confuted by arguments derived from the nature of existing things. With the devoutest submission to the law of Christ, they united an intrepid spirit of enquiry as to the correctest mode of acting in particular instances of conduct that occur among men. Assuming the doctrines of the Messiah concerning benevolence and justice for the regulation of their actions, they could not be persuaded to acknowledge that there was apparent in the divine code any prescribed rule whereby, for its own sake, one action rather than another, as fulfilling the will of their great Master, should be preferred.

The contempt with which the magistracy and priesthood regarded this obscure community of speculators had hitherto protected them from persecution. But they had arrived at that precise degree of eminence and prosperity which is peculiarly obnoxious to the hostility of the rich and powerful. The moment of their departure from Jerusalem was the crisis of their future destiny. Had they continued to seek a precarious refuge in a city of the Roman empire, this persecution would not have delayed to impress a new character on their opinions and their conduct; narrow views and the illiberality of sectarian patriotism would not have failed speedily to obliterate the magnificence and beauty of their wild and wonderful condition.

Attached from principle to peace, despising and hating the pleasures and the customs of the degenerate mass of mankind, this unostentatious community of good and happy men fled to the solitudes of Lebanon. To Arabians and enthusiasts the solemnity and grandeur of these desolate recesses possessed peculiar attractions. It well accorded with the justice of their conceptions on the relative duties of man towards his fellow in society that they should labour in unconstrained equality to dispossess the wolf and the tiger of their empire and establish on its ruins the dominion of intelligence and virtue. No longer would the worshippers of the God of Nature be indebted to a hundred hands for the accommodation of their simple wants. No longer would the poison of a diseased civilization embrue their very nutriment with pestilence. They would no longer owe their very existence to the vices, the fears, and the follies of mankind. Love, friendship, and philanthropy would now be the characteristic disposers of their industry. It is for his mistress or his friend that the labourer consecrates his toil; others are mindful, but he is forgetful, of himself. 'God feeds the hungry ravens, and clothes the lilies of the fields, and yet Solomon in all his glory is not like to one of these.'

Rome was now the shadow of her former self. The light of her grandeur and loveliness had passed away. The latest and the noblest of her poets and historians had foretold in agony her approaching slavery and degradation. The ruins of the human mind, more awful and portentous than the desolation of the most solemn temples, threw a shade of gloom upon her golden palaces which the brutal vulgar could not see, but which the mighty felt with inward trepidation and despair. The ruins of Jerusalem lay defenceless and uninhabited upon the burning sands; none visited, but in the depth of solemn awe, this accursed and solitary spot. Tradition says that there was seen to linger among the scorched and shattered fragments of the temple, one being, whom he that saw dared not to call man, with clasped hands, immovable eyes, and a visage horribly serene. Not on the will of the capricious multitude, nor the constant fluctuations of the many and the weak, depends the change of empires and religions. These are the mere insensible elements from which a subtler intelligence moulds its enduring statuary. They that direct the changes of this mortal scene breathe the decrees of their dominion from a throne of darkness and of tempest. The power of man is great.

After many days of wandering the Assassins pitched their tents in the valley of Bethzatanai. For ages had this fertile valley lain concealed from the adventurous search of man among mountains of everlasting snow. The men of elder days had inhabited this spot. Piles of monumental marble and fragments of columns that in their integrity almost seemed the work of some intelligence more sportive and fantastic than the gross conceptions of mortality, lay in heaps beside the lake and were visible beneath its transparent waves. The flowering orange-tree, the balsam, and innumerable odoriferous shrubs grew wild in the desolated portals. The fountain tanks had overflowed; and, amid the luxuriant vegetation of their margin, the yellow snake held its unmolested dwelling. Hither came the tiger and the bear to contend for those once domestic animals who had forgotten the secure servitude of their ancestors. No sound, when the famished beast of prey had retreated in despair from the awful desolation of this place, at whose completion he had assisted, but the shrill cry of the stork, and the flapping of his heavy wings from the capital of the solitary column, and the scream of the hungry vulture baffled of its only victim. The lore of ancient wisdom was sculptured in mystic characters on the rocks. The human spirit and the human hand had been busy here to accomplish its profoundest miracles. It was a temple dedicated to the God of knowledge and of truth. The palaces of the Caliphs and the Caesars might easily surpass these ruins in magnitude and sumptuousness; but they were the design of tyrants and the work of slaves. Piercing genius and consummate prudence had planned and executed Bethzatanai. There was deep and important meaning in every lineament of its fantastic sculpture. The unintelligible legend, once so beautiful and perfect, so full of poetry and history, spoke, even in destruction, volumes of mysterious import and obscure significance.

But in the season of its utmost prosperity and magnificence, art might not aspire to vie with nature in the valley of Bethzatanai. All that was wonderful and lovely was collected in this deep seclusion. The fluctuating elements seemed to have been rendered everlastingly permanent in forms of wonder and delight. The mountains of Lebanon had been divided to their base to form this happy valley; on every side their icy summits darted their white pinnacles into the clear blue sky, imaging, in their grotesque outline, minarets, and ruined domes, and columns worn with time. Far below the silver clouds rolled their bright volumes in many beautiful shapes and fed the eternal springs that, spanning the dark chasms like a thousand radiant rainbows, leaped into the quiet vale, then, lingering in many a dark glade among the groves of cypress and of palm, lost themselves in the lake. The immensity of these precipitous mountains, with their starry pyramids of snow, excluded the sun, which overtopped not, even in its meridian, their overhanging rocks. But a more heavenly and serener light was reflected from their icy mirrors, which, piercing through the many-tinted clouds, produced lights and colours of inexhaustible variety. The herbage was perpetually verdant and clothed the darkest recesses of the caverns and the woods.

Nature, undisturbed, had become an enchantress in these solitudes; she had collected here all that was wonderful and divine from the armoury of her omnipotence. The very winds breathed health and renovation and the joyousness of youthful courage. Fountains of crystalline water played perpetually among the aromatic flowers and mingled a freshness with their odour. The pine boughs became instruments of exquisite contrivance, among which every varying breeze waked music of new and more delightful melody. Meteoric shapes, more effulgent than the moonlight, hung on the wandering clouds and mixed in discordant dance around the spiral fountains. Blue vapours assumed strange lineaments under the rocks and among the ruins, lingering like ghosts with slow and solemn step. Through a dark chasm to the east, in the long perspective of a portal glittering with the unnumbered riches of the subterranean world, shone the broad moon, pouring in one yellow unbroken stream her horizontal beams. Nearer the icy region, autumn and spring held an alternate reign. The sere leaves fell and choked the sluggish brooks; the chilling fogs hung diamonds on every spray; and in the dark cold evening the howling winds made melancholy music in the trees. Far above shone the bright throne of winter, clear, cold, and dazzling. Sometimes there was seen the snowflakes to fall before the sinking orb of the beamless sun, like a shower of fiery sulphur. The cataracts, arrested in their course, seemed with their transparent columns to support the dark-browed rocks. Sometimes the icy whirlwind scooped the powdery snow aloft to mingle with the hissing meteors, and scatter spangles through the rare and rayless atmosphere.

Such strange scenes of chaotic confusion and harrowing sublimity, surrounding and shutting in the vale, added to the delights of its secure and voluptuous tranquillity. No spectator could have refused to believe that some spirit of great intelligence and power had hallowed these wild and beautiful solitudes to a deep and solemn mystery.

The immediate effect of such a scene, suddenly presented to the contemplation of mortal eyes, is seldom the subject of authentic record. The coldest slave of custom cannot fail to recollect some few moments in which the breath of spring or the crowding clouds of sunset, with the pale moon shining through their fleecy skirts, or the song of some lonely bird perched on the only tree of an unfrequented heath, has awakened the touch of nature. And they were Arabians who entered the valley of Bethzatanai – men who idolized nature and the God of nature, to whom love and lofty thoughts and the apprehensions of an uncorrupted spirit were sustenance and life. Thus securely excluded from an abhorred world, all thought of its judgement was cancelled by the rapidity of their fervid imaginations. They ceased to acknowledge, or deigned not to advert to, the distinctions with which the majority of base and vulgar minds control the longings and struggles of the soul towards its place of rest. A new and sacred fire was kindled in their hearts and sparkled in their eyes. Every gesture, every feature, the minutest action was modelled to beneficence and beauty by the holy inspiration that had descended on their searching spirits. The epidemic transport communicated itself through every heart with the rapidity of a blast from heaven. They were already disembodied spirits; they were already the inhabitants of paradise. To live, to breathe, to move was itself a sensation of immeasurable transport. Every new contemplation of the condition of his nature brought to the happy enthusiast an added measure of delight and impelled to every organ where mind is united with external things a keener and more exquisite perception of all that they contain of lovely and divine. To love, to be loved, suddenly became an insatiable famine of his nature, which the wide circle of the universe, comprehending beings of such inexhaustible variety and stupendous magnitude of excellence, appeared too narrow and confined to satiate.

Alas, that these visitings of the spirit of life should fluctuate and pass away! That the moments when the human mind is commensurate with all that it can conceive of excellent and powerful should not endure with its existence and survive its most momentous change! But the beauty of a vernal sunset, with its overhanging curtains of empurpled cloud, is rapidly dissolved to return at some unexpected period and spread an alleviating melancholy over the dark vigils of despair.

It is true the enthusiasm of overwhelming transport which had inspired every breast among the Assassins is no more. The necessity of daily occupation and the ordinariness of that human life, the burthen of which it is the destiny of every human being to bear had smothered, not extinguished, that divine and eternal fire. Not the less indelible and permanent were the impressions communicated to all; not the more unalterably were the features of their social character modelled and determined by its influence . . .

Love reborn

5 Church Terrace Pancrass London
October 3. 1814.

My dear Friend,

After a silence of some months I hasten to communicate to you the events of the interval. They will surprise, & if any degree of our ancient affection is yet cherished by you for a being apparently so inconsistent & indisciplinable as me, will probably delight you. You will rejoice that after struggles & privation which almost withered me to idiotism, I enjoy an happiness the most perfect & exalted that it is possible for my nature to participate. That I am restored to energy and enterprise, that I have become again what I once promised to become . . . that my friendship will no longer be an enigma to my friend, you will rejoice . . . If the causes that produced my errors have not made you indifferent to this reformation, & my restoration to peace, liberty & virtue.

As soon as I returned from the Continent (for I have travelled thro' France, Switzerland, Germany & Holland) I sought you to communicate what I will now detail.

In the beginning of Spring, I spent two months at Mrs Boinville's without my wife. If I except the succeeding period these two months were probably the happiest of my life: the calmest, the serenest, the most free from care. The contemplation of female excellence is the favourite food of my imagination. There was ample scope for admiration: novelty added a peculiar charm to the intrinsic merit of the objects: I had been unaccustomed to the mildness, the intelligence, the delicacy of a cultivated female. The presence of Mrs Boinville & her daughter afforded a strange contrast to my former friendship & deplorable condition. I suddenly perceived that the entire devotion with which I had resigned all prospects of utility or happiness to the single purpose of cultivating Harriet was a gross & despicable superstition. Perhaps every degree of affectionate intimacy with a female, however slight, partakes of the nature of love. Love makes men quick-sighted, & is only called blind by the multitude because he perceives the existence of relations invisible to grosser spirits. I saw the full extent of the calamity which my rash & heartless union with Harriet: an union over whose entrance might just be inscribed

'Lasciate ogni speranza, voi ch'entrate!'*

had produced. I felt as if a dead & living body had been linked together in loathsome & horrible communion. It was no longer possible to practise self deception: I believed that one revolting duty yet remained, to continue to deceive my wife. I wandered in the fields alone. The season was most beautiful. The evenings were so serene & mild. I had never before felt so intensely the subduing voluptuousness of the impulses of spring. Manifestation of my approaching change tinged my waking thoughts, & afforded inexhaustible subject for the visions of my sleep. I recollect that one day I undertook to walk from Bracknell to my father's, (40 miles). A train of visionary events arranged themselves in my imagination until ideas almost acquired the intensity of sensations. Already I had met the female, who was destined to be mine, already had replied to my exulting recognition, already were the difficulties surmounted that opposed an entire union. I had even proceeded so far as to compose a letter to Harriet on the subject of my passion for another. Thus was my walk beguiled, at the conclusion of which I was hardly sensible of fatigue.

In the month of June I came to London to accomplish some business with Godwin that had been long depending. The circumstances of the case required an almost constant residence at his house. There I met his daughter Mary. The originality & loveliness of Mary's character was apparent to me from her very motions & tones of voice. The irresistible

* 'Abandon hope, all you who enter here!' – Dante, *Inferno* [ed.]

wildness & sublimity of her feelings shewed itself in her gestures & her looks – Her smile, how persuasive it was, & how
pathetic! She is gentle, to be convinced & tender; yet not
incapable of ardent indignation & hatred. I do not think that
there is an excellence at which human nature can arrive, that
she does not indisputably possess, or of which her character
does not afford manifest intimations. I speak thus of Mary
now . . . and so intimately are our natures now united, that
I feel whilst I describe her excellencies as if I were an egoist
expatiating upon his own perfections. *Then*, how deeply did
I not feel my inferiority, how willingly confess myself far
surpassed in originality, in genuine elevation & magnificence
of the intellectual nature until she consented to share her capa-
bilities with me. I speedily conceived an ardent passion to
possess this inestimable treasure. In my own mind this feeling
assumed a variety of shapes, I disguised from myself the true
nature of my affection. I endeavoured also to conceal it from
Mary, but without success. I was vacillating & infirm of
purpose. I shuddered to transgress a real duty, & could not
in this instance perceive the boundaries by which virtue was
separated from madness, *when* self devotion becomes the very
prodigality of idiotism. Her understanding was made clear
by a spirit that sees into the truth of things, my affections
preserved pure & sacred from the corrupting contamination
of vulgar superstitions. No expressions can convey the re-
motest conception of the *manner* in which she dispelled my
delusions. The sublimer & rapturous moment when she confessed herself mine, who had so long been hers in secret,
cannot be painted to mortal imaginations. – Let it suffice to
you, who are my friend, to know & to rejoice that she is
mine: that at length I possess the inalienable treasure, that I
sought & I have found.

Tho' strictly watched, & regarded with a suspicious eye,
opportunities of frequent intercourse were not wanting.
When we meet, I will give you a more explicit detail of the
progress of our intercourse. How Godwin's distress induced
us to prolong the period of our departure. How the cruelty
& injustice with which we were treated, compelled us to
disregard all considerations but that of the happiness of each

other. We left England & proceeded to Switzerland & returned thro Germany & Holland. Two months have passed since this new state of being content. How wonderfully I am changed! Not a disembodied spirit can have undergone a stranger revolution! I never knew until now that contentment was anything but a word denoting an amusing abstraction. I never before felt the integrity of my nature, its various dependencies, & learned to consider myself as an whole accurately united – rather than an assemblage of inconsistent & discordant portions.

Above all, most sensibly do I perceive the truth of my entire worthlessness but as depending on another. And I am deeply persuaded that thus ennobled, I shall become a more true & constant friend, a more useful lover of mankind, a more ardent asserter of truth & virtue . . . above all more consistent, more intelligible, more true.

My dear friend I entreat you to write to me soon. Even in this pure & celestial felicity I am not contented until I hear from you.

Most affectionately yours P. B. Shelley.

3

Second Marriage

.

Introduction

THIS SECTION COVERS the remaining years of Shelley's life with Mary in England, a period of growing stability and domestic happiness, between 1815 and 1818. They lived for the most part outside London, in a series of small country houses near Bishopsgate and Marlow in the Thames Valley (rather than the valley of Bethzatanai). In spring 1815 he was bequeathed a £1,000 annuity on the death of his grandfather which gave him a substantial, if not aristocratic, independence; in 1816 little Willmouse was born, and his poetry received public recognition in Leigh Hunt's famous article on the new 'Young Poets'. He made the acquaintance of the other leading literary figures of his generation – Lord Byron, John Keats, William Hazlitt, Charles Lamb. He published two new volumes of poetry, *Alastor* (1816) and *The Revolt of Islam* (1817), while even more remarkably Mary published her own anonymous best-seller, *Frankenstein, or The Modern Prometheus* (1818). His household also successfully weathered a series of crises which might have broken up a less resilient group. Claire had a tempestuous affair with Byron which ended in the birth of an illegitimate daughter, Allegra, whom Shelley generously and tactfully absorbed into his own family (while keeping Claire by him despite Mary's protests). Mary's older half-sister Fanny committed suicide, followed a few weeks later by Harriet; and the Chancery Court case over the custody of Charles and Ianthe dragged on till the end of 1817.

But Shelley's writings on love show little reflection of these external stresses at this time: they emerge only later, in Italy. Instead they are calmer, more meditative and introspective than before: more self-questioning perhaps, but also more confident of being heard and appreciated. Almost everything he wrote at this time would have been shown to Mary, and probably to Claire also; and discussed at length. Interesting exceptions are the 'Constantia' poems to Claire, one of which Shelley secretly had published in *The Oxford Herald* without Mary's knowledge. The central theme that held Shelley was precisely the difficulty of domesticating passion, of overcoming destructive, adolescent 'self-centredness' in love, the fatal narcissism of the artist, and the seemingly insatiable drive to pursue the tantalizing woman of dreams in preference to the chosen woman of reality. For the modern reader it is perhaps helpful to see this inner struggle partly in psycho-analytic terms: Freud's 'pleasure principle' set against the 'reality principle'; or even more aptly, Jung's notion of the long, often harrowing process of subduing or coming to terms with the dark side of the Anima – the feminine principle – which leads to individuation and maturity. It is one of the most suggestive shortcomings of the early twentieth-century critics of Shelley – D. H. Lawrence, T. S. Eliot, Aldous Huxley, F. R. Leavis – who had admired him in their own adolescence, but subsequently turned against him, that they never realized how sharply and clearly this confrontation or inner struggle occurs in Shelley's writing. For them, Shelley never really escaped from the adolescent dream, the abstract narcissistic projection of the self. Yet the direct description and analysis of this profound and universal emotional dilemma becomes, from 1815 onwards, one of the most palpable themes of Shelley's writings on love. Why didn't his critics see this? First, I suspect, because they simply had not read his prose, or enough of his long poems apart from *Prometheus Unbound*. And second, because they themselves had such strong ideological views, and were each in their way such moralists about literature, that they could not – or would not – recognize what was most human, most commonplace, most vulnerable, and most tender-hearted about Shelley.

Thus the first extract begins as a personal plea for understanding and affection. It has been traditionally taken as addressed to Mary, and composed in his notebooks in the period 1814–15. 'If we reason, we would be understood; if we imagine, we would that the airy children of our brain were born anew within another's; if we feel, we would that another's nerves should vibrate to our own . . .' Characteristically, this appeal swiftly develops into a philosophical discussion of the *way* we all fall in love, of the natural impulse which 'thirsts after likeness', and the slow crystallization of the 'ideal prototype' of the beloved. (Shelley's terminology has been traced to Hume, Stewart and the Scottish School, but his notion of natural 'correspondence', 'vibration' and 'sympathy' is general among Romantic writers and can be found equally in Wordsworth and Coleridge.) What is most remarkable here, perhaps, is the emphasis Shelley lays not on ideal beauty or attractiveness in the beloved, but on the power of reciprocating feeling, on the depth of mutual understanding. What we all seek, he says, is 'an understanding capable of clearly estimating our own; an imagination which should enter into and seize upon the subtle and delicate peculiarities which we have delighted to cherish and unfold in secret.'

But how far is the 'ideal prototype' still essentially a narcissistic projection, a failure to recognize and respond to the 'otherness' of the beloved? This is the question which Shelley faces in the Preface to the poem *Alastor* and the central extract which follows. At Peacock's suggestion, Shelley took his title from the Greek, transliterating the word ἀlastvr: it is not the name of the doomed Poet-protagonist of the poem, but rather 'the evil spirit of solitude' – or self-obsession – which condemns him to search in vain for love. As Shelley puts it: 'He images to himself the Being whom he loves . . . (But) the Poet's self-centred seclusion was avenged by the furies of an irresistible passion pursuing him to speedy ruin.' Both Preface and poem were written at Bishopsgate in the autumn of 1815, at a period when Mary had temporarily excluded Claire from the household: but the shadows of both women move behind Shelley's visions. In the extract given, the Poet's search for his prototype continues to move (as in *The Assassins*) through an exotic, eastern landscape, but reaches a climax in a daring dream-sequence, clearly describing the sensations of sexual excitement rising to the point of orgasmic but illusory union, and then followed by dazed awakening, aching with the sense of loss and unfulfilled longing. For the modern reader *Alastor* is one of the most daring descriptions in all Romantic writing of the fascinating but destructive powers of the Anima, which will drive a person to wreck his life on fantasies, rather than commit himself to the daily responsibilities of love and affection. It is the first of three major poems on the theme of love, in which Shelley projected his experiences in symbolic, but increasingly confessional form, directly developing the prose material of his notebooks: the others are *Julian and Maddalo* (1818), and *Epipsychidion* (1821).

The section continues with two extracts in the polemic vein, returning to the question of marriage and free love. In the first, Shelley bitingly suggests that the marriage institution originated in the most primitive and brutal laws of property and possession, in which the male physically enforced his monopoly over 'the materials of usefulness or pleasure'. Thus marriage rests upon an ancient injustice, rather than a natural right. The position interestingly fore-shadows the socialist analysis by Engels in *The Origin of the Family, Private Property, and the State* (1884). In the next extract, he attacks the other extreme, pouring scorn on the idea that free love is simply an excuse for promiscuity. The passage is drawn from a book review of his friend Hogg's sensational novel *Prince Alexy Haimatoff* (1814), contributed to *The Critical Review*, and picking out the 'advanced' teaching of Prince Alexy's cynical old tutor Bruhle (who may be partly a satire on William Godwin). Shelley signed this article, and clearly approved of it; but in view of all the circumstances surrounding its publication, and also a certain naivete of style, it is my own guess that he secretly amused himself by getting Mary to write it, or at least part of it. Perhaps he intended to teach Hogg a proper attitude to 'reciprocity of duties' within the unconventional household in Chelsea, where Hogg joined Shelley, Mary and Claire for several weeks in the winter of 1814–15.

The section closes with a much longer extract from Shelley's notebook *Essay on Christianity*. With the exception of his purely political essay *A Philosophical View of Reform* (1820), this is perhaps the most unjustly neglected of all his original prose. It is the result of a sustained period of studying the Gospels and Acts of the Apostles at Bishopsgate and Marlow in 1816–17. Running through it is Shelley's continuing fascination with the ideals of primitive Christianity, and the sharing of love and property within a community. It may be a surprise to the modern reader to find him associating so closely the teachings of Jesus – the Jesus of the Gospels – with Rousseau; or to discover him emphasizing Universal Love as the ultimate principle opposed to materialism and injustice. However he now attacks the idea of the retired, pastoral community, attempting to isolate itself from society, and withdrawing itself from the process of social change and improvement: 'Rousseau certainly did not mean to persuade the immense population of his country to abandon all the arts of life, destroy their habitations and their temples, and become the inhabitants of the woods.' Equally, Shelley adopts a sympathetic but essentially rationalist attitude to the historical Jesus: he sees him as a great social and moral reformer (but not as a revolutionary), and in his teachings and parables as the greatest 'poet' of the transforming doctrine of Universal Love; while his miracles and divinity he regards as metaphors. He also characteristically places Christian doctrine within a comparative context of other world religions and philosophies, indicating its links with Mahometan and Platonic thought, and denying any divine originality. In all this Shelley again foreshadows a central nineteenth-century tradition, that of the rationalist historians and intellectual agnostics, summed up perhaps in Ernest Renan's *La Vie de Jésus* (1864).

All the writing of this period gives a sense of Shelley securing the ground of his emotional life, and seeking to define the problems of love more objectively. But at the same time there are premonitions of the storms to come. Meanwhile the *Essay on Christianity* points forward to the much more detailed examination he was soon to give to the Greek and Platonic theories of love.

Essay on love

What is love? Ask him who lives, what is life? Ask him who adores, what is God?

I know not the internal constitution of other men, nor even yours whom I now address. I see that in some external attributes they resemble me, but when misled by that appearance I have thought to appeal to something in common and unburden my inmost soul to them, I have found my language misunderstood like one in a distant and savage land. The more opportunities they have afforded me for experience, the wider has appeared the interval between us, and to a greater distance have the points of sympathy been withdrawn. With a spirit ill fitted to sustain such proof, trembling and feeble through its tenderness, I have everywhere sought sympathy and found only repulse and disappointment.

Thou demandest, What is Love? It is that powerful attraction towards all that we conceive, or fear, or hope beyond ourselves, when we find within our own thoughts the chasm of an insufficient void and seek to awaken in all things that are a community with what we experience within ourselves. If we reason, we would be understood; if we imagine, we would that the airy children of our brain were born anew within another's; if we feel, we would that another's nerves should vibrate to our own, that the beams of their eyes should kindle at once and mix and melt into our own, that lips of motionless ice should not reply to lips quivering and burning with the heart's best blood. This is Love. This is the bond and the sanction which connects not only man with man but with everything which exists. We are born into the world, and there is something within us which, from the instant that we live, more and more thirsts after its likeness. It is probably in correspondence with this law that the infant drains milk from the bosom of its mother; this propensity develops itself with the development of our nature. We dimly see within our intellectual nature a miniature as it were of our entire self, yet deprived of all that we condemn or despise, the ideal prototype of every thing excellent or lovely that we are capable of conceiving as belonging to the nature of man. Not only the portrait of our external being but an assemblage of the minutest particles of which our nature is composed;* a mirror whose surface reflects only the forms of purity and brightness; a soul within our soul that describes a circle around its proper paradise which pain, and sorrow, and evil dare not overleap. To this we eagerly refer all sensations, thirsting that they should resemble or correspond with it. The discovery of its anti-type; the meeting with an understanding capable of clearly estimating our own; an imagination which should enter into and seize upon the subtle and delicate peculiarities which we have delighted to cherish and unfold in secret; with a frame whose nerves, like the chords of two exquisite lyres, strung to the accompaniment of one delightful voice, vibrate with the vibrations of our own; and of a combination of all these in such proportion as the type within demands; this is the invisible and unattainable point to which Love tends; and to attain which, it urges forth the powers of man to arrest the faintest shadow of that without the possession of which there is no rest nor respite to the heart over which it rules. Hence in solitude, or in that deserted state when we are surrounded by human beings, and yet they sympathize not with us, we love the flowers, the grass, and the waters, and the sky. In the motion of the very leaves of spring, in the blue air, there is then found a secret correspondence with our heart. There is eloquence in the tongueless wind, and a melody in the flowing brooks and the rustling of the reeds beside them, which by their inconceivable relation to something within the soul, awaken the spirits to a dance of breathless rapture, and bring tears of mysterious tenderness to the eyes, like the enthusiasm of patriotic suc-

---

* 'These words are ineffectual and metaphorical. Most words are so – No help!' [*Shelley's note*]

cess, or the voice of one beloved singing to you alone. Sterne says that, if he were in a desert, he would love some cypress. So soon as this want or power is dead, man becomes the living sepulchre of himself, and what yet survives is the mere husk of what once he was.

Against solitude and self-centred love

The poem entitled *Alastor* may be considered as allegorical of one of the most interesting situations of the human mind. It represents a youth of uncorrupted feelings and adventurous genius led forth by an imagination inflamed and purified through familiarity with all that is excellent and majestic, to the contemplation of the universe. He drinks deep of the fountains of knowledge, and is still insatiate. The magnificence and beauty of the external world sinks profoundly into the frame of his conceptions, and affords to their modifications a variety not to be exhausted. So long as it is possible for his desires to point towards objects thus infinite and unmeasured, he is joyous, and tranquil, and self-possessed. But the period arrives when these objects cease to suffice. His mind is at length suddenly awakened and thirsts for intercourse with an intelligence similar to itself. He images to himself the Being whom he loves. Conversant with speculations of the sublimest and most perfect natures, the vision in which he embodies his own imaginations unites all of wonderful, or wise, or beautiful, which the poet, the philosopher, or the lover could depicture. The intellectual faculties, the imagination, the functions of sense, have their respective requisitions on the sympathy of corresponding powers in other human beings. The Poet is represented as uniting these requisitions, and attaching them to a single image. He seeks in vain for a prototype of his conception. Blasted by his disappointment, he descends to an untimely grave.

The picture is not barren of instruction to actual men. The Poet's self-centred seclusion was avenged by the furies of an irresistible passion pursuing him to speedy ruin. But that Power which strikes the luminaries of the world with sudden darkness and extinction, by awakening them to too exquisite a perception of its influences, dooms to a slow and poisonous decay those meaner spirits that dare to abjure its dominion. Their destiny is more abject and inglorious as their delinquency is more contemptible and pernicious. They who, deluded by no generous error, instigated by no sacred thirst of doubtful knowledge, duped by no illustrious superstition, loving nothing on this earth, and cherishing no hopes beyond, yet keep aloof from sympathies with their kind, rejoicing neither in human joy nor mourning with human grief; these, and such as they, have their apportioned curse. They languish, because none feel with them their common nature. They are morally dead. They are neither friends, nor lovers, nor fathers, nor citizens of the world, nor benefactors of their country. Among those who attempt to exist without human sympathy, the pure and tender-hearted perish through the intensity and passion of their search after its communities, when the vacancy of their spirit suddenly makes itself felt. All else, selfish, blind, and torpid, are those unforeseeing multitudes who constitute, together with their own, the lasting misery and loneliness of the world. Those who love not their fellow-beings live unfruitful lives, and prepare for their old age a miserable grave.

> 'The good die first,
> And those whose hearts are dry as summer dust,
> Burn to the socket!'

December 14, 1815

Nondum amabam, et amare amabam, quaerebam quid amarem, amans amare. – *Confess. St August.*

from Alastor

or The Spirit of Solitude

> . . . When early youth had passed, he left
> His cold fireside and alienated home
> To seek strange truths in undiscovered lands.
> Many a wide waste and tangled wilderness
> Has lured his fearless steps; and he has bought
> With his sweet voice and eyes, from savage men,
> His rest and food. Nature's most secret steps
> He like her shadow has pursued, where'er
> The red volcano overcanopies
> Its fields of snow and pinnacles of ice
> With burning smoke, or where bitumen lakes
> On black bare pointed islets ever beat
> With sluggish surge, or where the secret caves
> Rugged and dark, winding among the springs
> Of fire and poison, inaccessible
> To avarice or pride, their starry domes
> Of diamond and of gold expand above
> Numberless and immeasurable halls,
> Frequent with crystal column, and clear shrines
> Of pearl, and thrones radiant with chrysolite.
> Nor had that scene of ampler majesty
> Than gems or gold, the varying roof of heaven
> And the green earth lost in his heart its claims
> To love and wonder; he would linger long
> In lonesome vales, making the wild his home,
> Until the doves and squirrels would partake
> From his innocuous hand his bloodless food,
> Lured by the gentle meaning of his looks,
> And the wild antelope, that starts whene'er
> The dry leaf rustles in the brake, suspend
> Her timid steps to gaze upon a form

[75–105]

More graceful than her own.
                    His wandering step
Obedient to high thoughts, has visited
The awful ruins of the days of old:
Athens, and Tyre, and Balbec, and the waste
Where stood Jerusalem, the fallen towers
Of Babylon, the eternal pyramids,
Memphis and Thebes, and whatsoe'er of strange
Sculptured on alabaster obelisk,
Or jasper tomb, or mutilated sphynx,
Dark Æthiopia in her desert hills
Conceals. Among the ruined temples there,
Stupendous columns, and wild images
Of more than man, where marble daemons watch
The Zodiac's brazen mystery, and dead men
Hang their mute thoughts on the mute walls around,
He lingered, poring on memorials
Of the world's youth, through the long burning day
Gazed on those speechless shapes, nor, when the moon
Filled the mysterious halls with floating shades
Suspended he that task, but ever gazed
And gazed, till meaning on his vacant mind
Flashed like strong inspiration, and he saw
The thrilling secrets of the birth of time.

    Meanwhile an Arab maiden brought his food,
Her daily portion, from her father's tent,
And spread her matting for his couch, and stole
From duties and repose to tend his steps: –
Enamoured, yet not daring for deep awe
To speak her love: – and watched his nightly sleep,
Sleepless herself, to gaze upon his lips
Parted in slumber, whence the regular breath
Of innocent dreams arose: then, when red morn
Made paler the pale moon, to her cold home
Wildered, and wan, and panting, she returned.

    The Poet wandering on, through Arabie
And Persia, and the wild Carmanian waste,

[106–141]

And o'er the aërial mountains which pour down
Indus and Oxus from their icy caves,
In joy and exultation held his way;
Till in the vale of Cashmire, far within
Its loneliest dell, where odorous plants entwine
Beneath the hollow rocks a natural bower,
Beside a sparkling rivulet he stretched
His languid limbs. A vision on his sleep
There came, a dream of hopes that never yet
Had flushed his cheek. He dreamed a veilèd maid
Sate near him, talking in low solemn tones.
Her voice was like the voice of his own soul
Heard in the calm of thought; its music long,
Like woven sounds of streams and breezes, held
His inmost sense suspended in its web
Of many-coloured woof and shifting hues.
Knowledge and truth and virtue were her theme,
And lofty hopes of divine liberty,
Thoughts the most dear to him, and poesy,
Herself a poet. Soon the solemn mood
Of her pure mind kindled through all her frame
A permeating fire: wild numbers then
She raised, with voice stifled in tremulous sobs
Subdued by its own pathos: her fair hands
Were bare alone, sweeping from some strange harp
Strange symphony, and in their branching veins
The eloquent blood told an ineffable tale.
The beating of her heart was heard to fill
The pauses of her music, and her breath
Tumultuously accorded with those fits
Of intermitted song. Sudden she rose,
As if her heart impatiently endured
Its bursting burthen: at the sound he turned,
And saw by the warm light of their own life
Her glowing limbs beneath the sinuous veil
Of woven wind, her outspread arms now bare,
Her dark locks floating in the breath of night,
Her beamy bending eyes, her parted lips
Outstretched, and pale, and quivering eagerly.

[142–180]

His strong heart sunk and sickened with excess
Of love. He reared his shuddering limbs and quelled
His gasping breath, and spread his arms to meet
Her panting bosom: . . . she drew back a while,
Then, yielding to the irresistible joy,
With frantic gesture and short breathless cry
Folded his frame in her dissolving arms.
Now blackness veiled his dizzy eyes, and night
Involved and swallowed up the vision; sleep,
Like a dark flood suspended in its course,
Rolled back its impulse on his vacant brain.

Roused by the shock he started from his trance –
The cold white light of morning, the blue moon
Low in the west, the clear and garish hills,
The distinct valley and the vacant woods,
Spread round him where he stood. Whither have fled
The hues of heaven that canopied his bower
Of yesternight? The sounds that soothed his sleep,
The mystery and the majesty of Earth,
The joy, the exultation? His wan eyes
Gaze on the empty scene as vacantly
As ocean's moon looks on the moon in heaven.
The spirit of sweet human love has sent
A vision to the sleep of him who spurned
Her choicest gifts. He eagerly pursues
Beyond the realms of dream that fleeting shade;
He overleaps the bounds. Alas! Alas!
Were limbs, and breath, and being intertwined
Thus treacherously? Lost, lost, for ever lost,
In the wide pathless desert of dim sleep,
That beautiful shape! . . .

Women as property

Before the commencement of human society, if such a state can be conceived to have existed, it is probable that men like other animals used promiscuous concubinage. Force or persuasion regulated the particular instances of this general practice. No moral affections arose from the indulgence of a physical impulse; nor did the relations of parent and child endure longer than is essential for the preservation of the latter. The circumstance of the pleasure being attached to the fulfilment of the sexual functions rendered that which was the object of their exercise a possession analogous in value to those articles of luxury or necessity which maintain or delight the existence of a savage. The superiority of strength inherent in the male rendered him the possessor and the female the possession in the same manner as beasts are the property of men through their pre-eminence of reason and never are the property of each other through the inequality of opportunity and the success of fraud. Women, therefore, in rude ages and in rude countries have been considered as the property of men, because they are the materials of usefulness or pleasure. They were valuable to them in the same manner as their flocks and herds were valuable, and it was as important to their interests that they should retain undisturbed possession. The same dread of insecurity which gave birth to those laws or opinions which defend the security of property suggested also the institution of marriage: that is, a contrivance to prevent others from deriving advantage from that which any individual has succeeded in pre-occupying. I am aware that this institution has undergone essential modifications from an infinite multitude of circumstances which it is unnecessary to enumerate: such [undubitably] was however the original spirit of marriage . . .

Against promiscuous love

. . . Prince Alexy is by no means an unnatural, although no common character. We think we can discern his counterpart in Alfieri's delineation of himself. The same propensities, the same ardent devotion to his purposes, the same chivalric and unproductive attachment to unbounded liberty characterize both. We are inclined to doubt whether the author has not attributed to his hero the doctrines of universal philanthropy in a spirit of profound and almost unsearchable irony; at least he appears biassed by no peculiar principles, and it were perhaps an insoluble enquiry whether any, and if any, what moral truth he designed to illustrate by his tale. Bruhle, the tutor of Alexy, is a character delineated with consummate skill; the power of intelligence and virtue over external deficiencies is forcibly exemplified. The calmness, patience, and magnanimity of this singular man are truly rare and admirable; his disinterestedness, his equanimity, his irresistible gentleness form a finished and delightful portrait. But we cannot regard his commendation to his pupil to indulge in promiscuous concubinage without horror and detestation. The author appears to deem the loveless intercourse of brutal appetite a venial offence against delicacy and virtue! He asserts that a transient connection with a cultivated female may contribute to form the heart without essentially vitiating the sensibilities. It is our duty to protest against so pernicious and disgusting an opinion. No man can rise pure from the poisonous embraces of a prostitute, or sinless from the desolated hopes of a confiding heart. Whatever may be the claims of chastity, whatever the advantages of simple and pure affection, these ties, these benefits are of equal obligation to either sex. Domestic relations depend for their integrity upon a complete reciprocity of duties . . .

On Jesus Christ's doctrines
of universal love and equality

. . . If there be no love among men, it is best that he who sees through the hollowness of their professions should fly from their society and suffice to his own soul. In wisdom he will thus lose nothing; in peace, he will gain everything. In proportion to the love existing among men, so will be the community of property and power. Among true and real friends all is common, and were ignorance and envy and superstition banished from the world, all mankind would be as friends. The only perfect and genuine republic is that which comprehends every living being. Those distinctions which have been artificially set up of nations and cities and families and religions are only general names expressing the abhorrence and contempt with which men blindly consider their fellowmen. I love my country; I love the city in which I was born, my parents and my wife and the children of my care, and to this city, this woman, and this nation, it is incumbent on me to do all the benefit in my power. To what do these distinctions point, but to an indirect denial of the duty which humanity imposes on you of doing every possible good to every individual under whatever denomination he may be comprehended, to whom you have the power of doing it. You ought to love all mankind, nay, every individual of mankind; you ought not to love the individuals of your domestic circle less, but to love those who exist beyond it, more. Once make the feelings of confidence and affection universal and the distinctions of property and power will vanish; nor are they to be abolished without substituting something equivalent in mischief to them, until all mankind shall acknowledge an entire community of rights. But, as the shades of night are dispelled by the faintest glimmerings of dawn, so shall the minutest progress of the benevolent feelings disperse in some degree the gloom of tyranny and slavery – ministers of mutual suspicion and abhorrence.

Your physical wants are few, while those of your mind and heart cannot be numbered or described from their multitude and complication. To secure the gratification of the former, men have made themselves the bond-slaves of each other. They have cultivated these meaner wants to so great an excess as to judge nothing valuable or desirable but what relates to their gratification. Hence has arisen a system of passions which loses sight of the end which they were originally awakened to attain. Fame, power, and gold are loved for their own sakes, are worshipped with a blind and habitual idolatry. The pageantry of empire and the fame of irresistible might is contemplated by its possessor with unmeaning complacency, without a retrospect to the properties which first made him consider them of value. It is from the cultivation of the most contemptible properties of human nature that the discord and torpor and [*blank*] by which the moral universe is disordered essentially depend. So long as these are the ties by which human society is connected, let it not be admired that they are fragile.

Before man can be free and equal and truly wise he must cast aside the chains of habit and superstition; he must strip sensuality of its pomp and selfishness of its excuses, and contemplate actions and objects as they really are. He will discover the wisdom of universal love. He will feel the meanness and the injustice of sacrificing the leisure and the liberty of his fellowmen to the indulgence of his physical appetites and becoming a party to their degradation by the consummation of his own. He will consider ευγενειας δε και δοξας προσκοσμηματα κακιας ειναι, μονην τε ορθην πολιτειαν ειναι την εν κοσμω.*

* Though it appears to be in the Platonic style, this quotation has so far proved untraceable, and may be of Shelley's own composition. In the Bodleian mss. Shelley has put an asterisk against the passage, but gives no corresponding footnote of his own. The sentence means 'that the additional adornments of high birth and fame are evils, and that the only true republic is one which is universal'. Compare with the fifth sentence of the extract. [*ed.*]

Such, with those differences only incidental to the age and the state of society in which they were promulgated, appear to have been the doctrines of Jesus Christ. It is not too much to assert that they have been the doctrines of every just and compassionate mind that ever speculated on the social nature of man. The dogma of the equality of mankind has been advocated with various success in different ages of the world. It was imperfectly understood, but a kind of instinct in its favour influenced considerably on the practice of ancient Greece and Rome. Attempts to establish usages founded on this dogma have been made in modern Europe, in several instances since the revival of literature and the arts. Rousseau has vindicated this opinion with all the eloquence of sincere and earnest faith and is perhaps the philosopher among the moderns who in the structure of his feelings and understanding resembles most nearly the mysterious sage of Judaea. It is impossible to read those passionate words in which Jesus Christ upbraids the pusillanimity and sensuality of mankind, without being strongly reminded of the more connected and systematic enthusiasm of Rousseau. 'No man,' says Jesus Christ, 'can serve two masters . . . Take, therefore, no thought for the morrow; for the morrow shall take thought for the things of itself. Sufficient unto the day is the evil thereof.' If we would profit by the wisdom of a sublime and poetical mind, we must beware of the vulgar error of interpreting literally every expression which it employs. Nothing can well be more remote from truth than the literal and strict construction of such expressions as Jesus Christ delivers, or than it were best for man that he should abandon all his acquirements in physical and intellectual science and depend on the spontaneous productions of Nature for his subsistence. Nothing is more obviously false than that the remedy for the inequality among men consists in their return to the condition of savages and beasts. Philosophy will never be understood if we approach the study of its mysteries with so narrow and illiberal conceptions of its universality. Rousseau certainly did not mean to persuade the immense population of his country to abandon all the arts of life, destroy their habitations and their temples and become the inhabitants

of the woods. He addressed the most enlightened of his com-
patriots, and endeavoured to persuade them to set the
example of a pure and simple life, by placing in the strongest
point of view his conceptions of the calamitous and diseased
aspect which, overgrown as it is with the vices of sensuality
and selfishness, is exhibited by civilized society. Nor can it
be believed that Jesus Christ endeavoured to prevail on the
inhabitants of Jerusalem neither to till their fields nor to frame
a shelter against the sky, nor to provide food for the morrow.
He simply exposes with the passionate rhetoric of enthusiastic
love towards all human beings the miseries and mischiefs of
that system which makes all things subservient to the subsistence of the material frame of man. He warns them that no
man can serve two masters, God and Mammon; that it is
impossible at once to be high-minded and just and wise, and
comply with the accustomed forms of human society, seek
honour, wealth, or empire either from the idolatry of habit or
as the direct instruments of sensual gratification. He instructs
them that clothing and food and shelter are not, as they suppose, the true end of human life, but only certain means to
be valued in proportion to their subserviency to that end.
These means it is the right of every human being to possess,
and that in the same degree. In this respect the fowls of the
air and the lilies of the field are examples for the imitation of
mankind. They are clothed and fed by the Universal God.
Permit, therefore, the spirit of this benignant principle to visit
your intellectual frame, or, in other words, become just and
pure. When you understand the degree of attention which
the requisitions of your physical nature demand, you will
perceive how little labour suffices for their satisfaction. Your
heavenly father knows that you have need of these things.
The universal Harmony or Reason which makes your passive
frame of thought its dwelling in proportion to the purity and
majesty of its nature, will instruct you, if you are willing to
attain that exalted condition, in what manner to possess all
the objects necessary for your material subsistence. All men
are invocated to become thus pure and happy. All men are
called to participation in the community of nature's gifts. The
man who has fewest bodily wants approaches nearest to the

divine nature. Satisfy these wants, at the cheapest rate, and expend the remaining energies of your nature in the attainment of virtue and knowledge. The mighty frame of the wonderful and lovely world is the food of your contemplation, and living beings who resemble your own nature and are bound to you by similarity of sensations are destined to be the nutriment of your affections; united they are the consummation of the widest hopes that your mind can contain. You can expend thus no labour on mechanism consecrated to luxury and pride. How abundant will not be your progress in all that truly ennobles and extends human nature! By rendering yourselves thus worthy, you will be as free in your imaginations as the swift and many-coloured fowls of the air, and as beautiful in your simplicity as the lilies of the field.

In proportion as mankind becomes wise, yes, in exact proportion to that wisdom should be the extinction of the unequal system under which they now subsist. Government is in fact the mere badge of their depravity. They are so little aware of the inestimable benefits of mutual love as to indulge without thought and almost without motive in the worst excesses of selfishness and malice. Hence without graduating human society into a scale of empire and subjection, its very existence has become impossible. It is necessary that universal benevolence should supersede the regulations of precedent and prescription before these regulations can safely be abolished. Meanwhile their very subsistence depends on the system of injustice and violence which they have been devised to palliate. They suppose men endowed with the power of deliberating and determining for their equals; while these men, as frail and as ignorant as the multitude whom they rule, possess, as a practical consequence of this power, the right which they of necessity exercise to pervert, together with their own the physical and moral and intellectual nature of all mankind. It is the object of wisdom to equalize the distinctions on which this power depends, by exhibiting in their proper worthlessness the objects, a contention concerning which renders its existence a necessary evil. The evil in fact is virtually abolished wherever *justice* is practised, and it is abolished in precise proportion to the prevalence of true virtue. The whole frame of human things is infected by the insidious poison. Hence it is that man is blind in his understanding, corrupt in his moral sense, and diseased in his physical functions. The wisest and most sublime of the ancient poets saw this truth and embodied their conception of its value in retrospect to the earliest ages of mankind. They represented equality as the reign of Saturn and taught that mankind had gradually degenerated from the virtue which enabled them to enjoy or maintain this happy state. Their doctrine was philosophically false. Later and more correct observations have instructed us that uncivilized man is the most pernicious and miserable of beings and that the violence and injustice which are the genuine indications of real inequality obtain in the society of these beings without mixture and without palliation. Their imaginations of a happier state of human society were referred indeed to the Saturnian period; they ministered indeed to thoughts of despondency and sorrow. But they were the children of airy hope, the prophets and parents of mysterious futurity. Man was once as a wild beast; he has become a moralist, a metaphysician, a poet, and an astronomer. Lucretius or Virgil might have referred the comparison to themselves, and, as a proof of this progress of the nature of man, challenged a comparison with the cannibals of Scythia.* The experience of the ages which have intervened between the present period and that in which Jesus Christ taught tends to prove his doctrine and to illustrate theirs. There is more equality, because there is more justice among mankind and there is more justice because there is more universal knowledge.

To the accomplishment of such mighty hopes were the views of Jesus Christ extended; such did he believe to be the tendency of his doctrines; the abolition of artificial distinctions among mankind so far as the love which it becomes all human beings to bear towards each other, and the knowledge

* Jesus Christ foresaw what these poets retrospectively imagined. [*Shelley's note*]

of truth from which that love will never fail to be produced avail to their destruction.

A young man came to Jesus Christ struck by the miraculous dignity and simplicity of his character and attracted by the words of power which he uttered. He demanded to be considered as one of the followers of his creed. 'Sell all that thou hast,' replied the philosopher, 'give it to the poor, and follow me.' But the young man had large possessions, and he [. . .]

The system of equality was attempted, after Jesus Christ's death, to be carried into effect by his followers. 'They that believed had all things common: they sold their possessions and goods and parted them to all men as every man had need, and they continued daily with one accord in the temple and breaking bread from house to house did eat their meat with gladness and singleness of heart.'* The practical application of the doctrines of strict justice to a state of society established in its contempt was such as might have been expected. After the transitory glow of enthusiasm had faded from the minds of men, precedent and habit resumed their empire, broke like a universal deluge on one shrinking and solitary island. Men to whom birth had allotted these possessions looked with complacency on sumptuous apartments and luxurious food, and those ceremonials of delusive majesty which surround the throne of power and the court of wealth. Men from whom these things were withheld by their condition began again to gaze with stupid envy on their pernicious splendour and, by desiring the false greatness of another's state, to sacrifice the intrinsic majesty of their own. The demagogues of the infant republic of the Christian sect attaining through eloquence or artifice to influence among its members, first violated, under the pretence of watching over their integrity, the institutions established for the common and equal benefit of all. These demagogues artfully silenced the voice of the moral sense among them by engaging them to attend not so much to the cultivation of a virtuous and happy life in this mortal scene as to the attainment of a fortunate condition

---

* Acts, chap. 2, v. 44. [*Shelley's note*]

after death; not so much to the consideration of those means by which the state of man is adorned and improved as an enquiry into the secrets of the connection between God and the world, things which they well knew were not to be explained or even to be conceived. The system of equality which they established necessarily fell to the ground, because it is a system that must result from rather than precede the moral improvement of human kind. It was a circumstance of no moment that the first adherents of the system of Jesus Christ cast their property into a common stock. The same degree of real community of property could have subsisted without this formality, which served only to extend a temptation of dishonesty to the treasures of so considerable a patrimony. Every man in proportion to his virtue considers himself with respect to the great community of mankind as the steward and guardian of their interests in the property which he chances to possess. Every man in proportion to his wisdom sees the manner in which it is his duty to employ the resources which the consent of mankind has entrusted to his discretion. Such is the annihilation of the unjust inequality of powers and conditions existing in the world, so gradually and inevitably is the progress of equality accommodated to the progress of wisdom and of virtue among mankind. Meanwhile some benefit has not failed to flow from the imperfect attempts which have been made to erect a system of equal rights to property and power upon the basis of arbitrary institutions. They have undoubtedly in every case, from the very instability of their foundation, failed. Still they constitute a record of those epochs at which a true sense of justice suggested itself to the understandings of men so that they consented to forgo all the cherished delights of luxury, all the habitual gratifications arising out of the possession or the expectations of power, all the superstitions which the accumulated authority of ages had made dear and venerable to them. They are so many trophies erected in the enemy's land to mark the limits of the victorious progress of truth and justice. [. . .]

* * *

[. . .] The preachers of the Christian religion urge the morality of Jesus Christ as being itself miraculous and stamped with the impression of divinity. Mahomet advanced the same pretensions respecting the composition of the Koran and, if we consider the number of his followers, with greater success. But these gentlemen condemn themselves, for in their admiration they prefer the comment to the text. Read the words themselves of this extraordinary person, and weigh their import well. The doctrines indeed, in my judgement, are excellent and strike at the root of moral evil. If acted upon, no political or religious institution could subsist a moment. Every man would be his own magistrate and priest; the change so long desired would have attained its consummation, and man exempt from the external evils of his own choice would be left free to struggle with the physical evils which exist in spite of him. But these are the very doctrines which, in another shape, the most violent asserters of Christianity denounce as impious and seditious; who are such earnest champions for social and political disqualification as they? This alone would be a demonstration of the falsehood of Christianity, that the religion so called is the strongest ally and bulwark of that system of successful force and fraud and of the selfish passions from which it has derived its origin and permanence, against which Jesus Christ declared the most uncompromising war, and the extinction of which appears to have been the great motive of his life. We are called upon to believe in the divinity of a doctrine the effect of which has been to establish more firmly that which it was promulgated to destroy, and that they who invite us to [. . .] our reason with envious priests and tyrannical princes, whose existence is an everlasting answer to the pretensions of Christianity. Doctrines of reform were never carried to so great a length as by Jesus Christ. The *Republic* of Plato and the *Political Justice* of Godwin are probable and practical systems in the comparison.

The doctrines of Jesus Christ though excellent are not new. The immortality of the soul was already a dogma, familiar from all antiquity to every nation of the earth except the Jews. Plato said all that could be said on this subject, and whoever had aspired to excel this mighty mind ought to have sought their information from undoubted sources. Jesus claimed no pretension of the kind, and the Christian knows as little, as did the Pagan, of the foundation of this notion. The idea of forgiveness of injuries, the error of revenge, and the immorality and inutility of punishment considered as punishment, (for these correlative doctrines) are stated by Plato in the first book of the *Republic*; and . . .

[*the manuscript breaks off*]

4

Platonic Harmonies

Introduction

SHELLEY LEFT ENGLAND for the last time in March 1818, when he was still only 25. He gave his friends many explanations: the Chancery Case, sundry debts, ill-health, lack of literary recognition. More important were family considerations: little Allegra had to be delivered to Byron; he wanted to give his own children a freer upbringing, at least until they were of age for schools or tutors; and above all it would be much easier for Mary and Claire to remain outside English society until he had inherited the title and income on his father's death, which was thought to be imminent. (In fact Sir Timothy Shelley lived comfortably until 1844.) But underneath all this, Shelley was restless once again, and that old dream of the Mediterranean South, of sunshine and civilization, the fine arts and the instinctual life, which has continued to haunt English writers down to D. H. Lawrence, Aldous Huxley, Lawrence Durrell and John Fowles had thrown its enchantment over Shelley.

His translation of Plato's *Symposium* (which he preferred to call, more appreciatively, *The Banquet*) and his substantial essay on the Greek attitude to love both belong to this first radiant summer in Italy, and have an air of serenity and light which he never really attained again. The work was done in July and August, while Shelley was staying in a little stone cottage high up in the chestnut woods of the North Italian Apennines, above the remote country spa of Bagni di Lucca, in Tuscany. His household was small. Allegra had been dispatched with their Swiss nurse Elise to Byron at Venice, Clara and Willmouse were well, Mary in delightful humour, and Claire subdued and riding horses. The letters and diaries of this brief idyllic interlude show them picnicking in the woods, bathing in the freezing mountain streams, playing chess and reading together, and sometimes dancing in the evenings at the little provincial Casino of the Bagni.

Their cottage, the Casa Bertini, had a tiny tree-lined garden at the back (which still exists to this day), with a view of the glittering Lima far below in the valley; and here beneath the chequered shade of an ancient laurel bush Shelley worked each morning on Plato. He completed the first draft of the translation in ten days, which partly accounts for its fluency and grace. He had beside him a copy of Scapula's *Greek Lexicon*, and also a borrowed Latin version of the text by the Italian Renaissance scholar and philosopher Marsilio Ficino. Mary clean-copied the manuscript as he wrote, and the three of them discussed it in the evenings. Out of these shared talks about the Platonic philosophy, and the assumptions of the Greek society about the nature of love – heterosexual or homosexual – upon which historically it is based, Shelley conceived the idea of the introductory essay or *Discourse*, which he completed in a further two weeks in August. Overall, the concentrated intensity of his work is similar to that achieved in some of the later Italian poems – *Adonais, The Witch of Atlas*, and *Epipsychidion* – though the Platonic writing is in a special sense a communal effort.

Shelley's *Discourse* was written, he says, to 'enable the reader to form a liberal, consistent, and just judgement of the peculiarities of (Greek) domestic matters.' Though he begins by praising the Greek arts, he soon goes on to criticize the ancient Greek attitude to 'the regulations and the sentiments respecting sexual intercourse'. He sees Greek homosexuality as based on a social injustice as glaring as that of Greek slavery: the failure to treat and educate women as equal citizens. 'The fact is, that the modern Europeans have in this circumstance, and in the abolition of slavery, made an improvement the most decisive in the regulation of human society . . .' At the same time, in order to estimate the Greeks justly, Shelley takes the opportunity to give by comparison his own views on enlightened sexual behaviour. He writes here more explicitly, on physical matters, than anywhere else in his prose, and this is the chief interest of the *Discourse*.

The reader will make his own assessment, but once again

I think he will be struck by Shelley's apparent remoteness from modern attitudes, his mixture of delicacy and freedom. 'The act itself is nothing', he remarks, thereby separating himself from an entire literature of sexual performance and technique. The three guidelines he suggests are those of harmonious beauty, temperance in pleasure, and accordance with nature. Moreover everything he says tends not to reduce and isolate sexual activity, but to expand and integrate it: 'Man is in his wildest state a social being: a certain degree of civilization and refinement ever produces the want of sympathies still more intimate and complete; and the gratification of the senses is no longer all that is sought in sexual connection. It soon becomes a very small part of that profound and complicated sentiment, which we call Love, which is rather the universal thirst for a communion not merely of the senses, but of our whole nature, intellectual, imaginative and sensitive; and which, when individualized, becomes an imperious necessity . . .' In a post-Freudian society we may be as far from a Shelleyan view of sex, as Shelley was from the Greek view: yet Shelley sees love and sex together with a wholeness and a harmony which we can perhaps envy and regret.

Shelley's translation of the *Symposium*, which is given in full, does not require a detailed commentary here, except to make clear what a daring and remarkable production it was for its time, and how greatly it added to the value of his overall view of love. It is, surprisingly, only the second significant version to appear anywhere in English; and the earlier one (1792), by the Cambridge scholar Thomas Taylor, does not bear comparison. Plato's *Republic* had been a favoured teaching text ever since the Cromwellian Revolution; but the *Symposium* had been neglected because of its homosexual assumptions, and it was not a recommended work for Literae Humaniores at Oxford, for example, until 1847. It was typical of Shelley's boldness in the investigation of love that he becomes the first major English writer to attempt an objective account of Platonic homosexuality; and even more, through his introductory essay, and the poetic phrasing of his translation, to demonstrate that Plato's conception of love has a universal application, equally – and perhaps even more – relevant to a modern European and predominantly heterosexual culture, whose great limitation was not slavery, but materialism.

Shelley never prepared a final text for publication, and there are passages which lack polish. Mary submitted a heavily edited version for the *Complete Works* of 1840, but the entire translation did not appear until 1910, when for some two decades it became the standard version printed in the Everyman Library's collection of Platonic Dialogues; then once more it lapsed into obscurity. Yet Shelley's translation retains an ease and naturalness almost never recaptured in later, more scholarly, versions. His elegant but intellectual prose style seems almost perfectly suited to catch the Platonic combination of philosophic theorizing, witty logical interchange, and sudden radiant moments of poetry. His triumphs are the great set speeches of Pausanias, Agathon, and Socrates; and in a different vein, the acute comic parable of Aristophanes. The reader may recognize several themes already apparent in Shelley's own writings, and may wonder with what a delighted shock of recognition they also struck the rapt translator in the garden at Casa Bertini: love as a force of moral enquiry and improvement; love as the power that unites the subtly divided sexual nature of every being; love as the pursuit of the ideal form; and love as the mysterious impulse which makes men creative, and thereby godlike and free. Above all, Shelley infuses a sense of personal involvement into each aspect of the debate, with a graceful, playful earnestness that somehow retains the atmosphere of those long summer evenings with Mary and Claire, the talk moving back and forth under the Italian stars, and the echoes of other voices – Byron, Godwin, Keats – vibrating softly in the margins of the emerging text.

Shelley's *Symposium* has in fact a very special status in literary history. With the exception of Walter Savage Landor (who oddly enough was living nearby, at Pisa), Shelley was the best classicist of all the Romantic writers. His version of 1818 is thus *the* Romantic translation of Plato, just as Dr Benjamin Jowett's is the outstanding Victorian one (1871), and the representative modern text is probably the Penguin

Classics version by Walter Hamilton (1951). The interested reader will find the comparison between the three fascinating (there is even a case for a 'tri-lingual' edition), and will see how strongly each reflects, in prose rhythms, in nuance of vocabulary, and in emotional idiom – sudden moments of discretion, or candour – the three profoundly different types of English culture which brought them to birth. And also perhaps, three different notions of love in which they were conceived.

A Discourse on the Manners
of the Ancient Greeks
Relative to the Subject of Love

The period which intervened between the birth of Pericles and the death of Aristotle, is undoubtedly, whether considered in itself or with reference to the effects which it had produced upon the subsequent destinies of civilized man, the most memorable in the history of the world. What was the combination of moral and political circumstances which produced so unparalleled a progress during that short period in literature and the arts; – why that progress, so rapid and so sustained, so soon received a check, and became retrograde, – are problems left with the wonder and conjectures of posterity. The wrecks and fragments of those subtle and profound minds, like the ruins of a fine statue, obscurely suggest to us the grandeur and perfection of the whole. Their very language – a type of the understandings of which it was the creation and the image – in variety, in simplicity, in flexibility, and in copiousness, excels every other language of the western world. Their sculptures are such as we, in our presumption, assume to be the models of ideal truth and beauty, and to which no artist of modern times can produce forms in any degree comparable. Their paintings, according to Pliny and Pausanias, were full of delicacy and harmony; and some even were powerfully pathetic, so as to awaken, like tender music or tragic poetry, the most overwhelming emotions. We are accustomed to conceive of the painters of the sixteenth century, as those who have brought their art to the highest perfection, probably because none of the ancient paintings have been preserved. For all the inventive arts maintain, as it were, a sympathetic connection between each other, being no more than various expressions of one internal power, modified by different circumstances, either of an individual, or of society. The paintings of that period would probably bear the same relation as is confessedly borne by the sculptures to all succeeding ones. Of their music we know little; but the effects which it is said to have produced, whether they be attributed to the skill of the composer, or the sensibility of his audience, are far more powerful than any which we experience from the music of our own times; and if, indeed, the melody of their compositions were more tender and delicate, and inspiring, than the melodies of some modern European nations, their superiority in this art must have been something wonderful, and wholly beyond conception.

Their poetry seems also to maintain a very high, though not so disproportionate a rank, in the comparison. Perhaps Shakespeare, from the variety and comprehension of his genius, is to be considered, on a whole, as the greatest individual mind, of which we have specimens remaining. Perhaps Dante created imaginations of greater loveliness and energy than any that are to be found in the ancient literature of Greece. Perhaps nothing has been discovered in the fragments of the Greek lyric poets equivalent to the sublime and chivalric sensibility of Petrarch. – But, as a poet, Homer must be acknowledged to excel Shakespeare in the truth, the harmony, the sustained grandeur, the satisfying completeness of his images, their exact fitness to the illustration, and that to which they belong. Nor could Dante, deficient in conduct, plan, nature, variety, and temperance, have been brought into comparison with these men, but for those fortunate isles, laden with golden fruit, which alone could tempt any one to embark in the misty ocean of his dark and extravagant fiction.

But, omitting the comparison of individual minds, which can afford no general inference, how superior was the spirit and system of their poetry to that of any other period! So that, had any genius equal in other respects to the greatest that ever enlightened the world, arisen in that age, he would have been superior to all, from this circumstance alone – that his conceptions would have assumed a more harmonious and perfect form. For it is worthy of observation, that whatever the poets of that age produced is as harmonious and perfect as possible. If a drama, for instance, were the composition of a person of inferior talent, it was still homogeneous and free from inequalities; it was a whole, consistent with itself. The compositions of great minds bore throughout the sustained stamp of their greatness. In the poetry of succeeding ages the expectations are often exalted on Icarean wings, and fall, too much disappointed to give a memory and a name to the oblivious pool in which they fell.

In physical knowledge Aristotle and Theophrastus had already – no doubt assisted by the labours of those of their predecessors whom they criticize – made advances worthy of the maturity of science. The astonishing invention of geometry, that series of discoveries which have enabled man to command the elements and foresee future events, before the subjects of his ignorant wonder, and has opened as it were the doors of the mysteries of nature, had already been brought to great perfection. Metaphysics, the science of man's intimate nature, and logic, or the grammar and elementary principles of that science, received from the latter philosophers of the Periclean age a firm basis. All our more exact philosophy is built upon the labours of these great men, and many of the words which we employ in metaphysical distinctions were invented by them to give accuracy and system to their reasonings. The science of morals, or the voluntary conduct of men in relation to themselves or others, dates from this epoch. How inexpressibly bolder and more pure were the doctrines of those great men, in comparison with the timid maxims which prevail in the writings of the most esteemed modern moralists. They were such as Phocion, and Epaminondas, and Timoleon, who formed themselves on their influence, were to the wretched heroes of our own age.

Their political and religious institutions were more difficult to bring into comparison with those of other times. A summary idea may be formed of the worth of any political and religious system, by observing the comparative degree of happiness and of intellect produced under its influence. And whilst many institutions and opinions, which in ancient Greece were obstacles to the improvement of the human race, have been abolished among modern nations, how many pernicious superstitions and new contrivances of misrule, and unheard of complications of public mischief, have not been invented among them by the ever-watchful spirit of avarice and tyranny!

The modern nations of the civilized world owe the progress which they have made – as well in those physical sciences in which they have already excelled their masters, as in the moral and intellectual enquiries, in which, with all the advantage of their experience of the latter, it can scarcely be said that they have yet equalled them, – to what is called the revival of learning; that is, the study of the writers of the age which preceded and immediately followed the government of Pericles, or of subsequent writers, who were, so to speak, the rivers flowing from those immortal fountains. And though there seems to be a principle in the modern world, which, should circumstances analogous to those which modelled the intellectual resources of the age to which we refer, into so harmonious a proportion, again arise, would arrest and perpetuate them, and consign their results to a more equal, extensive, and lasting improvement of the condition of man – though justice and the true meaning of human society is, if not more accurately, more generally understood; though perhaps men know more, and therefore are more, as a mass, yet this principle has never been called into action, and requires indeed a universal and almost appalling change in the system of existing things. The study of modern history is the study of kings, financiers, statesmen, and priests. The history of ancient Greece is the study of legislators, philosophers, and poets; it is the history of men, compared with the history of titles. What the Greeks were, was a reality, not a promise. And what we are and hope to be, is derived, as it were, from the influence and inspiration of these glorious generations.

Whatever tends to afford a further illustration of the manners and opinions of those to whom we owe so much, and who were perhaps, on the whole, the most perfect specimens of humanity of whom we have authentic record, were infinitely valuable. Let us see their errors, their weaknesses, their daily actions, their familiar conversation, and catch the tone of their society. When we discover how far the most admirable community ever formed, was removed from that perfection to which human society is impelled by some active power within each bosom, to aspire, how great ought to be our hopes, how resolute our struggles! For the Greeks of the Periclean Age were widely different from us. It is to be lamented that no modern writer has hitherto dared to show them precisely as they were. Barthelemy cannot be denied the praise of industry and system; but he never forgets that he is a Christian and a Frenchman. Wieland, in his delightful novels, makes indeed a very tolerable Pagan, but cherishes too many political prejudices, and refrains from diminishing the interest of his romances by painting sentiments in which no European of modern times can possibly sympathize. There is no book which shows the Greeks precisely as they were; they seem all written for children, with the caution that no practice or sentiment, highly inconsistent with our present manners, should be mentioned, lest those manners should receive outrage and violation. But there are many to whom the Greek language is inaccessible, who ought not to be excluded by this prudery to possess an exact and comprehensive conception of the history of man; for there is no knowledge concerning what man has been and may be, from partaking of which a person can depart, without becoming in some degree more philosophical, tolerant, and just.

One of the chief distinctions between the manners of ancient Greece and modern Europe, consisted in the regulations and the sentiments respecting sexual intercourse. Whether this difference arises from some imperfect influence of the doctrines of Jesus Christ, who alleges the absolute and unconditional equality of all human beings, or from the institutions of chivalry, or from a certain fundamental difference of physical nature existing in the Celts, or from a combination of all or any of these causes, acting on each other, is a question worthy of voluminous investigation. The fact is, that the modern Europeans have in this circumstance, and in the abolition of slavery, made an improvement the most decisive in the regulation of human society; and all the virtue and the wisdom of the Periclean age arose under other institutions, in spite of the diminution which personal slavery and the inferiority of women, recognized by law and by opinions, must have produced in the delicacy, the strength, the comprehensiveness, and the accuracy of their conceptions, in moral, political, and metaphysical science, and perhaps in every other art and science.

The women, thus degraded, became such as it was expected that they should become. They possessed, except with extraordinary exceptions, the habits and the qualities of slaves. They were probably not extremely beautiful; at least there was no such disproportion in the attractions of the external form between the female and male sex among the Greeks, as exists among the modern Europeans. They were certainly devoid of that moral and intellectual loveliness with which the acquisition of knowledge and the cultivation of sentiment animates, as with another life of overpowering grace, the lineaments and the gestures of every form which it inhabits. Their eyes could not have been deep and intricate from the workings of the mind, and could have entangled no heart in soul-enwoven labyrinths.

Let it not be imagined that because the Greeks were deprived of its legitimate object, they were incapable of sentimental love; and that this passion is the mere child of chivalry and the literature of modern times. This object, or its archetype, forever exists in the mind, which selects among those who resemble it, that which most resembles it; and instinctively fills up the interstices of the imperfect image, in the same manner as the imagination moulds and completes the shapes in clouds, or in the fire, into the resemblances of whatever form, animal, building, etc., happens to be present to it. Man is in his wildest state a social being: a certain degree of civilization and refinement ever produces the want of sympathies still more intimate and complete; and the gratification of the senses is no longer all that is sought in sexual connection. It soon becomes a very small part of that profound and complicated sentiment, which we call Love, which is rather the universal thirst for a communion not merely of the senses, but of our whole nature, intellectual, imaginative and sensitive; and which, when individualized, becomes an imperious necessity, only to be satisfied by the complete or partial, actual or supposed, fulfilment of its claims. This want grows more powerful in proportion to the development which our nature receives from civilization; for man never ceases to be a social being. The sexual impulse, which is only one, and often a small part of those claims, serves, from its obvious and external nature, as a kind of type or expression of the rest, as common basis, an acknowledged and visible link. Still it is a claim which even derives a strength not its own from the accessory circumstances which surround it, and one which our nature thirsts to satisfy. To estimate this, observe the degree of intensity and durability of the love of the male towards the female in animals and savages; and acknowledge all the duration and intensity observable in the love of civilized beings beyond that of savages to be produced from other causes. In the susceptibility of the external senses there is probably no important difference.

Among the ancient Greeks the male sex, one half of the human race, received the highest cultivation and refinement; whilst the other, so far as intellect is concerned, were educated as slaves, and were raised but few degrees in all that related to moral or intellectual excellence above the condition of savages. The gradations in the history of man present us with a slow improvement in this respect. The Roman women held a higher consideration in society, and were esteemed almost as the equal partners with their husbands in the regulation of domestic economy and the education of their children. The practices and customs of modern Europe are essentially different from and incomparably less pernicious than either, however remote from what an enlightened mind cannot fail to desire as the future destiny of human beings.

From this distinction arose that difference of manners which subsists between the ancient Greeks and the modern Europeans. They both had arrived at that epoch of refinement, when sentimental love becomes an imperious want of the heart and of the mind. The senses of both sought with the same impatient eagerness that gratification upon which the perpetuity of our species depends. In modern Europe the sexual and intellectual claims of love, by the more equal cultivation of the two sexes, so far converge towards one point, as to produce, in the attempt to unite them, no gross violation in the established nature of man.

Among the Greeks these feelings, being thus deprived of their natural object, sought a compensation and a substitute. The men of Greece corresponded in external form to the models which they have left as specimens of what they were. The firm yet flowing proportion of their forms, the winning unreserve and facility of their manners, the eloquence of their speech, in a language which is itself music and persuasion; their gestures animated at once with the delicacy and the boldness which the perpetual habit of persuading and governing themselves and others; and the poetry of their religious rites, inspired into their whole being, rendered the youth of Greece a race of beings something widely different from that of modern Europe. If my observation be correct, the word καλος (beautiful) is more frequently applied to the male sex, whilst ευειδης (handsome) denoted the attractiveness of a female. Whether the cause is to be sought in the climate, in the original constitution of the peculiar race of the Greeks, or in the institutions and system of society, or in the mutual action of these several circumstances, such is the effect. And as a consequence of those causes, beautiful persons of the male sex became the object of that sort of feelings, which are only cultivated at present as towards females.

An enlightened philosophy, although it must condemn the laws by which an indulgence in the sexual instinct is usually regulated, suggests, however, the propriety of habits of chastity in like manner with those of temperance. It regards the senses as but a minute and subordinate portion of our complicated nature, and it deems the pleasures to be derived from their exercise such as are rather weakened, not enhanced, by repetition, especially if unassociated with some principle from which they may participate in permanency and excellence. Few characters are more degraded than that of an habitual libertine; that is a person who is in the custom of seeking a relief from the impulse of the sexual instinct, divested of those associated sentiments which in a civilized state, precede, accompany, or follow such an act.

The act itself is nothing. The sources of condemnation to be pronounced against the indulgence in this gratification are twofold.

1st as it regards the complicated and arbitrary distinctions of society; and the other as it regards the indestructible laws of human nature.

With respect to the first, the one general law applicable to all other actions is applicable also to this: – that nothing is to be done, which, including your own being in the estimate, will produce, on the whole, greater pain than pleasure. In this sense adultery, seductions, etc., until mankind shall have enough. With respect to the second, the following propositions may be established as applications of this general law.

1st. That the person selected as the subject of this gratification should be as perfect and beautiful as possible, both in body and in mind; so that all sympathies may be harmoniously blended, and the moments of abandonment be prepared by the entire consent of all the conscious portions of our being; the perfection of intercourse consisting, not perhaps in a total annihilation of the instinctive sense, but in the reducing it to as minute a proportion as possible, compared with those higher faculties of our nature, from which it derives a value.

2ndly. Temperance in pleasure. This prevents the act which ought always to be the link and type of the highest emotions of our nature from degenerating into a diseased habit, equally pernicious to body and mind. Everyone will recollect Mrs Shandy's clock; and after the customary smile has past, cannot but be shocked at the picture it affords of the brutal prostitution of the most sacred impulses of our being.

3rdly. This act ought to be indulged *according to nature*. A volume of definitions and limitations belong to this maxim, which here may be passed over.

To apply these propositions to the Greeks. The passion which their poets and philosophers described and felt seems inconsistent with this latter maxim, in a degree inconceivable to the imagination of a modern European. But let us not exaggerate the matter. We are not exactly aware, – and the laws of modern composition scarcely permit a modest writer to investigate the subject with philosophical accuracy, – what that action was by which the Greeks expressed this passion. I am persuaded that it was totally different from the ridiculous and disgusting conceptions which the vulgar have formed on the subject, at least except among the more debased and abandoned of mankind. It is impossible that a lover could usually have subjected the object of his attachment to so detestable a violation or have consented to associate his own remembrance in the beloved mind with images of pain and horror. If we consider the facility with which certain phenomena connected with sleep, at the age of puberty, associate themselves with those images which are the objects of our waking desires; and even that in some persons of an exalted state of sensibility, that a similar process may take place in reverie, it will not be difficult to conceive the almost involuntary consequences of a state of abandonment in the society of a person of surpassing attractions, when the sexual connection cannot exist, to be such as to preclude the necessity of so operose and diabolical a machination as that usually described. This is the result apparently alluded to by Plato.* That it could seldom have approached to a resemblance with the vulgar imputation, even among the more gross and unrefined Romans, I appeal to a passage of Petronius, well known to every scholar, in which Giton, the pathic is represented to talk the language of a woman receiving pleasure from the embraces of Encolpius. This, even as a piece of meretricious flattery, is wholly inconsistent with the vulgar notion.

But let us not measure the Greeks of the age to which I refer, with our own feeble conceptions of the intensity of disinterested love; or according to the horrible commentary which the imitation of their manners by the licentious Romans who had contributed to the overthrow of the Republic, produced upon the text. Probably there were innumerable instances among that exalted and refined people, in which

* *Phaedrus*

never any circumstance happens [to] the lover and his beloved by which natural modesty was wronged. The lover appeased his physical instinct with his wife or his slave; or was engrossed in such lofty thoughts and feelings as admitted of no compromise between them and less intense emotions. Thus much is to be admitted, that, represent this passion as you will, there is something totally irreconcilable in its cultivation to the beautiful order of social life, to an equal participation in which all human beings have an indefeasible claim, and from which half of the human race, by the Greek arrangement, were excluded. This invidious distinction of human kind, as a class of beings of intellectual nature, into two sexes, is a remnant of savage barbarism which we have less excuse than they for not having totally abolished.

The action by which this passion was expressed, taken in its grossest sense, is indeed sufficiently detestable. But a person must be blinded by superstition to conceive of it as more horrible than the usual intercourse endured by almost every youth of England with a diseased and insensible prostitute. It cannot be more unnatural, for nothing defeats and violates nature, or the purposes for which the sexual instincts are supposed to have existed, than prostitution. Nor is it possible that the society into which the one plunges its victim should be more pernicious than the other. Nothing is at the same time more melancholy and ludicrous than to observe that the inhabitants of one epoch or of one nation, harden themselves to all amelioration of their own practices and institutions and soothe their consciences by heaping violent invectives upon those of others; while in the eye of sane philosophy their own are no less deserving of censure. If it be enquired how an individual ought to act in the [*blank*] – the reply is – make the best of a bad matter.

The ideas suggested by Catullus, Martial, Juvenal and Suetonius never occur among the Greeks; or even among those Romans, who, like Lucretius, Virgil, Horace, imitated them. The Romans were brutally obscene; the Greeks seemed hardly capable of obscenity in a strict sense. How innocent is even the *Lysistrata* of Aristophanes compared with the infamous perversions of Catullus! The earlier dramatic English writers are often frightfully obscene, exceeding even the Romans. I should consider obscenity to consist in a capability of associating disgusting images with the act of the sexual instinct. Luxury produced for the Romans what the venereal disease did for the writers of James, and after the redeeming interval over which Milton presided the effects of both were united, under Charles II, to infect literature.

It may blunt the harshness of censure also to reflect that in the golden age of our own literature a certain sentimental attachment towards persons of the same sex was not uncommon. Shakespeare has devoted the impassioned and profound poetry of his sonnets to commemorate an attachment of this kind, which we cannot question was wholly divested of any unworthy alloy. Towards the age of Charles II it is said that this romantic friendship degenerated into licentiousness and this latter age bears the same relation to the former as the first of the Roman Empire, to [. . .]

Thus far the translator has thought it his duty to overstep the jealous limits between what the learned and the unlearned know of the Greeks; and to indicate a system of reasoning which may enable the reader to form a liberal, consistent, and just judgement of the peculiarities of their domestic manners. This slight sketch was undertaken to induce the reader to cast off the cloak of his self-flattering prejudices and forbid the distinction of manners, which he has endeavoured to preserve in the translation of the ensuing piece, [to] interfere with his delight or his instruction.

On The Symposium

or Preface to the Banquet of Plato

A FRAGMENT

Plato is eminently the greatest among the Greek philosophers, and from him, or, rather, perhaps through him, from his master Socrates, have proceeded those emanations of moral and metaphysical knowledge, in which a long series and an incalculable variety of popular superstitions have sheltered their absurdities from the slow contempt of mankind. Plato exhibits the rare union of close and subtle logic, with the Pythian enthusiasm of poetry, melted by the splendour and harmony of his periods into one irresistible stream of musical impressions, which hurry the persuasions onward, as in a breathless career. His language is that of an immortal spirit, rather than a man. Lord Bacon is, perhaps, the only writer, who, in these particulars, can be compared with him: his imitator, Cicero, sinks in the comparison into an ape mocking the gestures of a man. His views into the nature of mind and existence are often obscure, only because they are profound; and though his theories respecting the government of the world, and the elementary laws of moral action, are not always correct, yet there is scarcely any of his treatises which do not, however stained by puerile sophisms, contain the most remarkable intuitions into all that can be the subject of the human mind. His excellence consists especially in intuition, and it is this faculty which raises him far above Aristotle, whose genius, though vivid and various, is obscured in comparison with that of Plato.

The dialogue entitled the Banquet was selected by the translator as the most beautiful and perfect among all the works of Plato. He despairs of having communicated to the English language any portion of the surpassing graces of the composition, or having done more than present an imperfect shadow of the language and the sentiment of this astonishing production.

It is called ερωτικος or a discussion upon Love, and is supposed to have taken place at the house of Agathon, at one of a series of festivals given by that poet, on the occasion of his gaining the prize of tragedy at the Dionysiaca. The account of the debate on this occasion is supposed to have been given by Apollodorus, a pupil of Socrates, many years after it had taken place, to a companion who was curious to hear it. This Apollodorus appears, both from the style in which he is represented in this piece, as from a passage in the *Phaedon*, to have been a person of an impassioned and enthusiastic disposition; to borrow an image from the Italian painters, he seems to have been the St John of the Socratic groups. The drama (for so the lively distinction of characters and the various and well-wrought circumstances of the story almost entitle it to be called) begins by Socrates persuading Aristodemus to sup at Agathon's, uninvited. The whole of this introduction affords the most lively conception of refined Athenian manners. [. . .]

The Symposium

or The Banquet, translated from Plato

THE PERSONS OF THE DIALOGUE
> APOLLODORUS
> A FRIEND OF APOLLODORUS
> GLAUCO
> ARISTODEMUS
> SOCRATES
> AGATHON
> PHAEDRUS
> PAUSANIAS
> ERYXIMACHUS
> ARISTOPHANES
> DIOTIMA
> ALCIBIADES

Apollodorus. I think that the subject of your enquiries is still fresh in my memory; for yesterday, as I chanced to be returning home from Phaleros, one of my acquaintance, seeing me before him, called out to me from a distance, jokingly, 'Apollodorus, you Phalerian, will you not wait a minute?' – I waited for him, and as soon as he overtook me, 'I have just been looking for you, Apollodorus,' he said, 'for I wished to hear what those discussions were on Love, which took place at the party, when Agathon, Socrates, Alcibiades, and some others met at supper. Some one who heard of them from Phoenix, the son of Philip, told me that you could give a full account, but he could relate nothing distinctly himself. Relate to me, then, I entreat you, all the circumstances. I know you are a faithful reporter of the discussions of your friend; but first tell me, were you present at the party or not?'

'Your informant,' I replied, 'seems to have given you no

very clear idea of what you wish to hear, if he thinks that these discussions took place so lately as that I could have been of the party.' – 'Indeed I thought so,' replied he. – 'For how,' said I, 'O Glauco! could I have been present? Do you not know that Agathon has been absent from the city many years? But since I began to converse with Socrates, and to observe each day all his words and actions, three years are scarcely past. Before this time I wandered about wherever it might chance, thinking that I did something, but being, in truth, a most miserable wretch, not less than you are now, who believe that you ought to do anything rather than practise the love of wisdom.' – 'Do not cavil,' interrupted Glauco, 'but tell me, when did this party take place?'

'Whilst we were yet children,' I replied, 'when Agathon first gained the prize of tragedy, and the day after that on which he and the chorus made sacrifices in celebration of their success.' – 'A long time ago, it seems. But who told you all the circumstances of the discussion? Did you hear them from Socrates himself?' 'No, by Jupiter, but the same person from whom Phoenix had his information, one Aristodemus, a Cydathenean, – a little man who always went about without sandals. He was present at this feast, being, I believe, more than any of his contemporaries, a lover and admirer of Socrates. I have questioned Socrates concerning some of the circumstances of his narration, who confirms all that I have heard from Aristodemus.' – 'Why then,' said Glauco, 'why not relate them, as we walk, to me? The road to the city is every way convenient, both for those who listen and those who speak.'

Thus as we walked, I gave him some account of those discussions concerning Love; since, as I said before, I remember them with sufficient accuracy. If I am required to relate them also to you, that shall willingly be done; for, whensoever either I myself talk of philosophy, or listen to others talking of it, in addition to the improvement which I conceive there arises from such conversation, I am delighted beyond measure; but whenever I hear your discussions about monied men and great proprietors, I am weighed down with grief, and pity you, who, doing nothing, believe that you are doing something. Perhaps you think that I am a miserable wretch; and, indeed, I believe that you think truly. I do not think, but well know, that you are miserable.

Companion. You are always the same, Apollodorus – always saying some ill of yourself and others. Indeed, you seem to me to think every one miserable except Socrates, beginning with yourself. I do not know what could have entitled you to the surname of the 'Madman', for, I am sure, you are consistent enough, forever inveighing with bitterness against yourself and all others, except Socrates.

Apollodorus. My dear friend, it is manifest that I am out of my wits from this alone – that I have such opinion as you describe concerning myself and you.

Companion. It is not worth while, Apollodorus, to dispute now about these things; but do what I entreat you, and relate to us what were these discussions.

Apollodorus. They were such as I will proceed to tell you. But let me attempt to relate them in the order which Aristodemus observed in relating them to me. He said that he met Socrates washed, and, contrary to his usual custom, sandalled, and having enquired whither he went so gaily dressed, Socrates replied, 'I am going to sup at Agathon's; yesterday I avoided it, disliking the crowd, which would attend at the prize sacrifices then celebrated; today I promised to be there, and I made myself so gay, because one ought to be beautiful to approach one who is beautiful. But you, Aristodemus, what think you of coming uninvited to supper?' 'I will do,' he replied, 'as you command.' 'Follow then, that we may, by changing its application, disarm that proverb, which says, *To the feasts of the good, the good come uninvited.* Homer, indeed, seems not only to destroy, but to outrage the proverb; for, describing Agamemnon as excellent in battle, and Menelaus but a faint-hearted warrior, he represents Menelaus as coming uninvited to the feast of one braver and better than himself.' – Aristodemus hearing this, said, 'I also am in some danger, Socrates, not as you say, but according to Homer, of approaching like an unworthy inferior the banquet of one more wise and excellent than myself. Will you not, then, make some excuse for me? for, I shall not confess that I came uninvited, but shall say that I was invited by you.' – 'As we walk together,' said Socrates, 'we will consider together what excuse to make – but let us go.'

Thus discoursing, they proceeded. But as they walked, Socrates, engaged in some deep contemplation, slackened his pace, and, observing Aristodemus waiting for him, he desired him to go on before. When Aristodemus arrived at Agathon's house he found the door open, and it occurred, somewhat comically, that a slave met him at the vestibule, and conducted him where he found the guests already reclined. As soon as Agathon saw him, 'You arrive just in time to sup with us, Aristodemus,' he said; 'if you have any other purpose in your visit, defer it to a better opportunity. I was looking for you yesterday, to invite you to be of our party; I could not find you anywhere. But how is it that you do not bring Socrates with you?'

But he turning round, and not seeing Socrates behind him, said to Agathon, 'I just came hither in his company, being invited by him to sup with you.' – 'You did well,' replied Agathon, 'to come; but where is Socrates?' – 'He just now came hither behind me; I myself wonder where he can be.' – 'Go and look, boy,' said Agathon, 'and bring Socrates in; meanwhile, you, Aristodemus, recline there near Eryximachus.' And he bade a slave wash his feet that he might recline. Another slave, meanwhile, brought word that Socrates had retired into a neighbouring vestibule, where he stood, and, in spite of his message, refused to come in. – 'What absurdity you talk!' cried Agathon; 'call him, and do not leave him till he comes.' – 'Leave him alone, by all means,' said Aristodemus; 'it is customary with him sometimes to retire in this way and stand wherever it may chance. He will come presently, I do not doubt; do not disturb him.' – 'Well, be it as you will,' said Agathon; 'as it is, you boys, bring supper for the rest; put before us what you will, for I resolved that there should be no master of the feast. Consider me and these my friends, as guests, whom you have invited to supper, and serve them so that we may commend you.'

After this they began supper, but Socrates did not come

in. Agathon ordered him to be called, but Aristodemus perpetually forbade it. At last he came in, much about the middle
of supper, not having delayed so long as was his custom.
Agathon (who happened to be reclining at the end of the
table, and alone,) said, as he entered, 'Come hither, Socrates,
and sit down by me; so that by the mere touch of one so
wise as you are, I may enjoy the fruit of thy meditations in
the vestibule; for, I well know, you would not have departed
till you had discovered and secured it.'

Socrates, having sat down as he was desired, replied, 'It
would be well, Agathon, if wisdom were of such a nature as
that when we touched each other, it would overflow of its
own accord, from him who possesses much to him who
possesses little; like the water in the two chalices, which will
flow through a flock of wool from the fuller into the emptier,
until both are equal. If wisdom had this property, I should
esteem myself most fortunate in reclining near to you. I
should thus soon be filled, I think, with the most beautiful
and various wisdom. Mine, indeed, is something obscure,
and doubtful, and dreamlike. But yours is radiant, and has
been crowned with amplest reward; for though you are yet
so young, it shone forth from you, and became so manifest
yesterday, that more than 30,000 Greeks can bear testimony
to its excellence and loveliness.' – 'You are laughing at me,
Socrates,' said Agathon; 'but you and I will decide this
controversy about wisdom by and bye, taking Bacchus for
our judge. At present turn to your supper.'

After Socrates and the rest had finished supper, and had
reclined back on their couches, and the libations had been
poured forth, and they had sung hymns to the God, and all
other rites which are customary had been performed, they
turned to drinking. Then Pausanias made this kind of proposal. 'Come, my friends,' said he, 'in what manner will it
be pleasantest for us to drink? I must confess to you that, in
reality, I am not very well from the wine we drank last night
and I have some need of intermission. I suspect that most of
you are in the same condition, for you were here yesterday.
Now, consider how we shall drink most easily and
comfortably.'

' 'Tis a good proposal, Pausanias,' said Aristophanes, 'to contrive, in some way or other, to place moderation in our cups. I was one of those who were drenched last night.' – Eryximachus, the son of Acumenus, hearing this, said: 'I am of your opinion; I only wish to know one thing – whether Agathon is in the humour for hard drinking?' – 'Not at all,' replied Agathon; 'I confess that I am not able to drink much this evening.' – 'It is an excellent thing for us,' replied Eryximachus – 'I mean myself, Aristodemus, Phaedrus, and these others – if you, who are such invincible drinkers, now refuse to drink. I ought to except Socrates, for he is capable of drinking everything or nothing; and whatever we shall determine will equally suit him. Since, then, no one present has any desire to drink much wine, I shall perhaps give less offence if I declare the nature of drunkenness. The science of medicine teaches us that drunkenness is very pernicious; nor would I willingly choose to drink immoderately myself, or counsel another to do so, especially if he had been drunk the night before.' – 'Yes,' said Phaedrus, the Myrinusian, interrupting him, 'I have been accustomed to confide in you, especially in your directions concerning medicine; and I would not willingly do so, if the rest will do the same.' All then agreed that they would drink at this present banquet not for drunkenness but for pleasure.

'Since, then,' said Eryximachus, 'it is decided that no one shall be compelled to drink more than he pleases, I think that we may as well send away the flute-player to play to herself; or, if she likes, to the women within. Let us devote the present occasion to conversation between ourselves, and if you wish, I will propose to you what shall be the subject of our discussions.' All present desired and entreated that he would explain. – 'The exordium of my speech,' said Eryximachus, 'will be in the style of the *Melanippe* of Euripides, for the story which I am about to tell belongs not to me, but to Phaedrus. Phaedrus has often indignantly complained to me, saying – "Is it not strange, Eryximachus, that there are innumerable hymns and paeans composed for the other Gods, but that not one of the many poets who spring up in the world has ever composed a verse in honour of Love, who is such and so great a God? Nor any one of those accomplished sophists, who, like the famous Prodicus, have celebrated the praise of Hercules and others, has ever celebrated that of Love; but what is more astonishing, I have lately met with the book of some philosopher, in which salt is extolled on account of its utility, and many other things of the same nature are in like manner celebrated with elaborate praise. That so much serious thought is expended on such trifles, and that no man has dared to this day to frame a hymn in honour of Love, who being so great a deity, is thus neglected, may well be sufficient to excite my indignation."

'There seemed to me some justice in these complaints of Phaedrus; I propose, therefore, at the same time, for the sake of giving pleasure to Phaedrus, and that we may on the present occasion do something well and befitting us, that this God should receive from those who are now present the honour which is most due to him. If you agree to my proposal, an excellent discussion might arise on the subject. Everyone ought, according to my plan, to praise Love with as much eloquence as he can. Let Phaedrus begin first, both because he reclines the first in order, and because he is the father of the discussion.'

'No one will vote against you, Eryximachus,' said Socrates, 'for how can I oppose your proposal, who am ready to confess that I know nothing on any subject but love? Or how can Agathon, or Pausanias, or even Aristophanes, whose life is one perpetual ministration to Venus and Bacchus? Or how can any other whom I see here? Though we who sit last are scarcely on an equality with you; for if those who speak before us shall have exhausted the subject with their eloquence and reasonings, our discourses will be superfluous. But in the name of Good Fortune, let Phaedrus begin and praise Love.' The whole party agreed to what Socrates said, and entreated Phaedrus to begin.

What each then said on this subject, Aristodemus did not entirely recollect, nor do I recollect all that he related to me; but only the speeches of those who said what was most worthy of remembrance. First, then, Phaedrus began thus:—

'Love is a mighty deity, and the object of admiration, both

to Gods and men, for many and for various claims; but especially on account of his origin. For that he is to be honoured as one of the most ancient of the Gods, this may serve as a testimony, that Love has no parents, nor is there any poet or other person who has ever affirmed that there are such. Hesiod says, that first "Chaos was produced; then the broad-bosomed Earth, to be a secure foundation for all things; then Love." He says that after Chaos these two were produced, the Earth and Love. Parmenides, speaking of generation, says: – "But he created Love before any of the Gods." Acusileus agrees with Hesiod. Love, therefore, is universally acknowledged to be among the eldest of things. And in addition to this, Love is the author of our greatest advantages; for I cannot imagine a greater happiness and advantage to one who is in the flower of youth than an amiable lover, or to a lover than an amiable object of his love. For neither birth, nor wealth, nor honours, can awaken in the minds of men the principles which should guide those who from their youth aspire to an honourable and excellent life, as Love awakens them. I speak of the fear of shame, which deters them from that which is disgraceful; and the love of glory which incites to honourable deeds. For it is not possible that a state or private person should accomplish, without these incitements, anything beautiful or great. I assert, then, that should one who loves be discovered in any dishonourable action, or tamely enduring insult through cowardice, he would feel more anguish and shame if observed by the object of his passion, than if he were observed by his father or his companions, or any other person. In like manner, one who is the object of love is especially grieved to be discovered by his lover in any dishonourable act. If then, by any contrivance, a state or army could be composed of lovers and the beloved, it is beyond calculation how excellently they would administer their affairs, refraining from any thing base, contending with each other for the acquirement of fame, and exhibiting such valour in battle as that, though few in numbers, they might subdue all mankind. For should a lover desert the ranks or cast away his arms in the presence of his beloved, he would suffer far acuter shame from that one person's regard, than from the regard of all other men. A thousand times would he prefer to die, rather than desert the object of his attachment, and not succour him in danger.

'There is none so worthless whom Love cannot impel, as it were, by a divine inspiration, towards virtue, even so that he may through this inspiration become equal to one who might naturally be more excellent; and, in truth, as Homer says: *The God breathes vigour into certain heroes* – so Love breathes into those who love, the spirit which is produced from himself. Not only men, but even women who love, are those alone who willingly expose themselves to die for others. Alcestis, the daughter of Pelias, affords to the Greeks a remarkable example of this opinion; she alone being willing to die for her husband, and so surpassing his parents in the affection with which love inspired her towards him, as to make them appear, in the comparison with her, strangers to their own child, and related to him merely in name; and so lovely and admirable did this action appear, not only to men, but even to the Gods, that, although they conceded the prerogative of bringing back the spirit from death to few among the many who then performed excellent and honourable deeds, yet, delighted with this action, they redeemed her soul from the infernal regions: so highly do the Gods honour zeal and devotion in love. They sent back indeed Orpheus, the son of Oeagrus, from Hell, with his purpose unfulfilled, and showing him only the spectre of her for whom he came, refused to render up herself. For Orpheus seemed to them, not as Alcestis, to have dared die for the sake of her whom he loved, and thus to secure to himself a perpetual intercourse with her in the regions to which she had preceded him, but like a cowardly musician, to have contrived to descend alive into Hell; and, indeed, they appointed as a punishment for his cowardice, that he should be put to death by women.

'Far otherwise did they regard Achilles, the son of Thetis, whom they sent to inhabit the islands of the blessed. For Achilles, though informed by his mother that his own death would ensue upon his killing Hector, but that if he refrained from it he might return home and die in old age, yet preferred revenging and honouring his beloved Patroclus; not to die for him merely, but to disdain and reject that life which he had ceased to share. Therefore the Gods honoured Achilles beyond all other men, because he thus preferred his friend to all things else. Aeschylus talks nonsense when he says, that Patroclus was beloved by Achilles, who was more beautiful, not only than Patroclus, but than all the other heroes, who was in the freshness of youth, and beardless, and according to Homer, much younger than his friend. But in truth the species of devotion in love which he exhibited is that which the Gods chiefly honour. Far more do they love and admire and crown with rewards the beloved who cherishes his lover, than the lover who cherishes his beloved; for the lover is diviner than the beloved, he is inspired by the God. On this account have they rewarded Achilles more amply than Alcestis; permitting his spirit to inhabit the islands of the blessed. Hence do I assert that Love is the most ancient and venerable of deities, and most powerful to endow mortals with the possession of happiness and virtue, both whilst they live and after they die.'

Thus Aristodemus reported the discourse of Phaedrus; and after Phaedrus, he said that some others spoke, whose discourses he did not well remember. When they had ceased, Pausanias began thus:–

'Simply to praise Love, O Phaedrus, seems to me too bounded a scope for our discourse. If Love were one, it would be well. But since Love is not one, I will endeavour to distinguish which is the Love whom it becomes us to praise, and having thus discriminated one from the other, will attempt to render him who is the subject of our discourse the honour due to his divinity. We all know that Venus is never without Love; and if Venus were one, Love would be one; but since there are two Venuses, of necessity also must there be two Loves. For assuredly are there two Venuses; one, the eldest, the daughter of Uranus, born without a mother, whom we call the Uranian; the other younger, the daughter of Jupiter and Dione, whom we call the Pandemian; – of necessity must there also be two Loves, the Uranian and Pandemian companions of these Goddesses. It is becoming to praise all the Gods, but the attributes which fall to the lot of each may be

distinguished and selected. For any particular action whatever, in itself is neither good nor evil; what we are now doing
– drinking, singing, talking, none of these things are good
in themselves, but the mode in which they are done stamps
them with its own nature; and that which is done well, is
good, and that which is done ill, is evil. Thus, not all love,
nor every mode of love is beautiful, or worthy of commendation, but that alone which excites us to love worthily. The
love, therefore, which attends upon Venus Pandemos is, in
truth, common to the vulgar, and presides over transient
and fortuitous connections, and is worshipped by the least
excellent of mankind: the votaries of this deity regard women
as equally objects of love with men; they seek the body rather
than the soul, and the ignorant rather than the wise, disdaining all that is honourable and lovely, and considering
how they shall best satisfy their sensual necessities. This Love
is derived from the younger Goddess, who partakes in her
nature both of male and female. But the attendant on the
other, the Uranian, whose nature is entirely masculine, is the
Love who inspires us with affection towards men, and
exempts us from all wantonness and libertinism. Those who
are inspired by this divinity seek the affections of that sex
which is endowed by nature with greater excellence and vigour both of body and mind. And it is easy to distinguish
those who especially exist under the influence of this power,
by their choosing in early youth as the objects of their love
those in whom the intellectual faculties have begun to
develop: in preference to mere youths. For those who begin
to love in this manner, seem to me to be preparing to pass
their whole life together in a community of good and evil,
and not ever lightly deceiving those who love them, to be
faithless to their vows. There ought to be a law that none
should love mere youths; so much serious affection as this
deity enkindles should not be doubtfully bestowed; for the
body and mind of those so young are yet unformed, and it
is difficult to foretell what will be their future tendencies and
power. The good voluntarily impose this law upon themselves, and those vulgar lovers ought to be compelled to the
same observance, as we deter them with all the power of the

laws from the love of free matrons. For these are persons whose shameful actions embolden those who observe their importunity and intemperance, to assert, that it is dishonourable to serve and gratify the objects of our love. But no one who does this gracefully and according to law, can justly be liable to the imputations of blame.

'The law as it relates to love in other cities may be easily understood, for it is plainly defined. Here and in Lacedaemon it is various. In Elis and in Boeotia, where men are yet unskilled in philosophy and the use of language, the law simply declares that it is honourable to serve those we love: nor has any legislator either of ancient or modern times considered it dishonourable for this reason I imagine, because unaware of these distinctions, they were unwilling to throw obstacles in their own way by a vain attempt to dissuade the youth wholly from this practice. In Ionia and many other places, which are subject to the Barbarians, the law declares this affectionate service to be shameful. For not only this species of love, but philosophy and the practice of the gymnastic exercises, are represented as dishonourable by the tyrannical governments under which the Barbarians live. For I imagine it would little conduce to the benefit of the governors, that the governed should be disciplined to lofty thoughts and to unity and communion of steadfast friendship, of which admirable effects the tyrants of our own country have also learned that Love is the author. For the love of Harmodius and Aristogiton, strengthened into a firm friendship, dissolved the tyranny. Wherever, therefore, it is declared dishonourable in any case to serve and benefit lovers, that law is a mark of the depravity of the legislator, and avarice and tyranny of the rulers, and the cowardice of those who are ruled. Wherever it is simply declared to be honourable without distinction of cases, such a declaration denotes dulness and want of subtlety of mind in the authors of the regulation. Here the degree of praise or blame to be attributed by law to this practice is far better regulated; but it is yet difficult to determine the cases to which they should refer.

'It is evident, however, for one in whom this passion is enkindled, it is more honourable to love openly than secretly;

and most honourable to love the most excellent and virtuous, even if they should be less beautiful than others. It is honourable for the lover to exhort and sustain the object of his love in virtuous conduct. It is considered honourable to attain the love of those whom we seek, and the contrary shameful; and to facilitate this attainment, the law has given to the lover the permission of acquiring favour by the most extraordinary devices, which if a person should practise for any purpose besides this, he would incur the severest reproof of philosophy. For if any one desirous of accumulating money, or ambitious of procuring power, or seeking any other advantage, should, like a lover, seeking to acquire the favour of his beloved, employ prayers and entreaties in his necessity, and swear such oaths as lovers swear, and sleep before the threshold, and offer to subject himself to such slavery as no slave even would endure; he would be frustrated of the attainment of what he sought, both by his enemies and friends; these reviling him for his flattery, those sharply admonishing him, and taking to themselves the shame of his servility. But there is a certain grace in a lover who does all these things, and the law declares that he alone may do them without dishonour. It is commonly said that the Gods accord pardon to the lover alone if he should break his oath, and that there is no oath by Venus. Thus as our law declares, both Gods and men have given to lovers all possible indulgence.

'Considering these things, how admirable a thing in the state is love, and the affection and the facility of lovers towards each other! But since on the other hand the fathers of those who are the objects of love command their masters not to suffer them to converse with their lovers, and their comrades reproach them, if they perceive any intimacy of that kind, and those who are old do not reproach the censurers as if they censured unjustly; considering these things I say, one might think that this species of service and attachment were held to be dishonourable.

'The affair, however, I imagine, stands thus: As I have before said, Love cannot be considered in itself as either honourable or dishonourable: if it is honourably pursued, it is honourable; if dishonourably, dishonourable: it is dishonourable basely to serve and gratify a worthless person; it is honourable honourably to serve a person of virtue. That Pandemic lover who loves rather the body than the soul, is worthless, nor can be constant and consistent, since he has placed his affections on that which has no stability. For as soon as the flower of the form, which was the sole object of his desire, has faded, then he departs and is seen no more; bound by no faith or shame of his many promises and persuasions. But he who is the lover of virtuous manners is constant during life, since he has placed himself in harmony and desire with that which is consistent with itself.

'These two classes of persons our law directs us to distinguish with careful examination, so that we may serve and converse with the one and avoid the other; determining, by that enquiry, by what the lover is attracted, and for what the object of his love is dear to him. On the same account it is considered dishonourable to be inspired with love at once, lest time should be wanting to know and approve the character of the object. It is considered dishonourable to be captivated by the allurements of wealth and power, or terrified through injuries to yield up the affections, or not to despise in the comparison with an unconstrained choice all political influence and personal advantage. For no circumstance is there in wealth or power so invariable and consistent, as that no generous friendship can ever spring up from amongst them. Our law therefore has left one method by which the beloved may gratify his lover. We have a law with respect to lovers which declares that it shall not be considered servile or disgraceful, though the lover should submit himself to any species of slavery for the sake of his beloved. The same opinion holds with respect to those who undergo any degradation for the sake of virtue. For it is esteemed among us, that if any one chooses to serve and obey another for the purpose of becoming more wise or more virtuous through the intercourse that might thence arise, such willing slavery is not the slavery of a dishonest flatterer. Through this law we should consider in the same light a servitude undertaken for the sake of love as one undertaken for the acquirement of wisdom or any other excellence, if indeed the devotion of a lover to his beloved is to be considered a beautiful thing. For when the lover and the beloved have once arrived at the same point, the province of each being distinguished; the one serving and gratifying his beloved, now his indeed in all things in which it were not unjust to serve him; the one conceding to his lover, the author of his wisdom and virtue, whatever it were not honourable to refuse; the one able to assist in the cultivation of the mind and in the acquirement of every other excellence; the other yet requiring education, and seeking the possession of wisdom; then alone, by the union of these conditions, and in no other case, is it honourable for the beloved to yield up his affections to his lover. In this servitude alone there is no disgrace in being deceived and defeated of the object for which it was undertaken; whereas every other is disgraceful, whether we are deceived or no. For if any one favours his lover for his wealth, and is deceived in the advantage which he expected, his lover turning out to be poor instead of rich, his conduct is not the less base; for such an one has already shown that for the sake of money he would submit in anything to any one. On the same principle, if any one favours another, believing him to be virtuous, for the sake of becoming better through the intercourse and affection for his lover, and is deceived; his lover turning out to be worthless, and far from the possession of virtue; yet it is honourable to have been so deceived. For such an one seems to have submitted to the servitude of Love, because he would endure anything from any one for the sake of becoming more virtuous and wise; a disposition of mind eminently beautiful.

'This is that Love who attends on the Uranian deity, and is Uranian; the author of innumerable benefits both to the state and to individuals, and by the necessity of whose influences both the lover and the beloved are disciplined into the zeal of virtue. All other Loves are the attendants on Venus Pandemos. So much, although unpremeditated, is what I have to deliver on the subject of love, O Phaedrus.'

Pausanias having ceased (for so the learned teach me to denote the changes of the discourse), Aristodemus said that it came to the turn of Aristophanes to speak; but it happened that, from repletion or some other cause, he had an hiccup which prevented him; so he turned to Eryximachus, the physician, who was reclining close beside him, and said – 'Eryximachus, it is but fair that you should cure my hiccup, or speak instead of me until it is over.' – 'I will do both,' said Eryximachus; 'I will speak in your turn, and you, when your hiccup has ceased, shall speak in mine. Meanwhile, if you hold your breath some time, it will subside. If not, gargle your throat with water; and if it still continues, take something to stimulate your nostrils, and sneeze; do this once or twice, and even though it should be very violent it will cease.' – 'Whilst you speak,' said Aristophanes, 'I will follow your directions.' – Eryximachus then began:–

'Since Pausanias, beginning his discourse excellently, placed no fit completion and development to it, I think it necessary to attempt to fill up what he has left unfinished. He has reasoned well in defining Love as of a double nature. The science of medicine, to which I have addicted myself, seems to teach me that the love which impels towards those who are beautiful, does not subsist only in the souls of men, but in the bodies also of those of all other living beings which are produced upon earth, and, in a word, in all things which are. So wonderful and mighty is this divinity, and so widely is his influence extended over all divine and human things! For the honour of my profession, I will begin by adducing a proof from medicine. The nature of the body contains within itself this double Love. For that which is healthy and that which is diseased in a body differ and are unlike: that which is unlike, loves and desires that which is unlike. Love, therefore, is different in a sane and in a diseased body. Pausanias has asserted rightly that it is honourable to gratify those things in the body which are good and healthy, and in this consists the skill of the physician; whilst those which are bad and diseased, ought to be treated with no indulgence. The science of medicine, in a word, is a knowledge of the love affairs of the body, as they bear relation to repletion and evacuation; and he is the most skilful physician who can trace in those operations the good and evil love, can make the one change places with the other, and attract love into those parts from which he is absent, or expel him from those which he ought not to occupy. He ought to make those things which are most inimical, friendly, and excite them to mutual love. But those things are most inimical, which are most opposite to each other: cold to heat, bitterness to sweetness, dryness to moisture. Our progenitor, Aesculapius, as the poets inform us, (and indeed I believe them,) thro' the skill which he possessed to inspire Love and concord in these contending principles, established the science of medicine.

'The gymnastic arts and agriculture, no less than medicine, are exercised under the dominion of this God. Music, as any one may perceive, who yields a very slight attention to the subject, originates from the same source; which Heraclitus probably meant, though he could not express his meaning very clearly in words, when he says, "One though apparently differing, yet so agrees with itself, as the harmony of a lyre and a bow." It is great absurdity to say that an harmony differs, and can exist between things whilst they are dissimilar; but probably he meant that from sounds which first differed, like the grave and the acute, and which afterwards agreed, harmony was produced according to musical art. For no harmony can arise from the grave and the acute whilst yet they differ. But harmony is symphony: symphony is, as it were, concord. But it is impossible that concord should subsist between things that differ, so long as they differ. Between things which are discordant and dissimilar there is then no harmony. A rhythm is produced from that which is quick, and that which is slow, first being distinguished and opposed to each other, and then made accordant; so does medicine, no less than music, establish a concord between the objects of its art, producing love and agreement between adverse things.

'Music is then the knowledge of that which relates to Love in harmony and rhythm. In the very system of harmony and rhythm, it is easy to distinguish love. The double Love is not distinguishable in music itself; but it is required to apply it to the service of mankind by rhythm and harmony, which is called poetry, or the composition of melody; or by the correct use of songs and measures already composed, which is called discipline; then one can be distinguished from the other, by the aid of an extremely skilful artist. And the better love ought to be honoured and preserved for the sake of those who are virtuous, and that the nature of the vicious may be changed through the inspiration of its spirit. This is that beautiful Uranian love, the attendant of the Uranian muse: the Pandemian is the attendant of Polyhymnia; to whose influence we should only so far subject ourselves, as to derive pleasure from it without indulging to excess; in the same manner as, according to our art, we are instructed to seek the pleasures of the table, only so far as we can enjoy them without the consequences of disease. In music, therefore, and in medicine, and in all other things, human and divine, this double Love ought to be traced and discriminated; for it is in all things.

'Even the constitution of the seasons of the year is penetrated with these contending principles. For so often as heat and cold, dryness and moisture, of which I spoke before, are influenced by the more benignant Love, and are harmoniously and temperately intermingled with the seasons, they bring maturity and health to men, and to all other animals and plants. But when the evil and injurious Love assumes the dominion of the seasons of the year, destruction is spread widely abroad. Then pestilence is accustomed to arise, and many other blights and diseases fall upon animals and plants: and hoar frosts, and hails, and mildew on the corn, are produced from that excessive and disorderly love, with which each season of the year is impelled towards the other; the motions of which and the knowledge of the stars, is called astronomy. All sacrifices, and all those things in which divination is concerned (for these things are the links by which is maintained an intercourse and communion between the Gods and men) are nothing else than the science of preservation and right government of Love. For impiety is accustomed to spring up, so soon as any one ceases to serve the more honourable Love, and worship him by the sacrifice of good actions; but submits himself to the influences of the other, in relation of his duties towards his parents, and the Gods, and the living, and the dead. It is the object of divination to distinguish and remedy the effects of these opposite Loves; and divination is therefore the author of the friendship of Gods and men, because it affords the knowledge of what in matters of Love is lawful or unlawful to men.

'Thus every species of Love possesses collectively a various and vast, or rather universal power. But Love which incites to the acquirement of its objects according to virtue and wisdom, possesses the most exclusive dominion, and prepares for his worshippers the highest happiness through the mutual intercourse of social kindness which it promotes among them, and through the benevolence which he attracts to them from the Gods, our superiors.

'Probably in thus praising Love, I have unwillingly omitted many things; but it is your business, O Aristophanes, to fill up all that I have left incomplete; or, if you have imagined any other mode of honouring the divinity; for I observe your hiccup is over.'

'Yes,' said Aristophanes, 'but not before I applied the sneezing. I wonder why the harmonious construction of our body should require such noisy operations as sneezing; for it ceased the moment I sneezed.' – 'Do you not observe what you do, my good Aristophanes?' said Eryximachus; 'you are going to speak, and you predispose us to laughter, and compel me to watch for the first ridiculous idea which you may start in your discourse, when you might have spoken in peace.' – 'Let me unsay what I have said, then,' replied Aristophanes, laughing. 'Do not watch me, I entreat you; though I am not afraid of saying what is laughable (since that would be all gain, and quite in the accustomed spirit of my muse) but lest I should say what is ridiculous.' – 'Do you think to throw your dart, and escape with impunity, Aristophanes? Attend, and what you say be careful you maintain; then, perhaps, if it pleases me, I may dismiss you without question.'

'Indeed, Eryximachus,' proceeded Aristophanes, 'I have designed that my discourse should be very different from yours and that of Pausanias. It seems to me that mankind are by no means penetrated with a conception of the power of Love, or they would have built sumptuous temples and altars, and have established magnificent rites of sacrifice in his honour; he deserves worship and homage more than all the other Gods, and he has yet received none. For Love is of all the Gods the most friendly to mortals; and the physician of those wounds, whose cure would be the greatest happiness which could be conferred upon the human race. I will endeavour to unfold to you his true power, and you can relate what I declare to others.

'You ought first to know the nature of man, and the adventures he has gone through; for his nature was anciently far different from that which it is at present. First, then, human beings were formerly not divided into two sexes, male and female; there was also a third, common to both the others, the name of which remains, though the sex itself has disappeared. The androgynous sex, both in appearance and in name, was common both to male and female; its name alone remains, which labours under a reproach.

'At the period to which I refer, the form of every human being was round, the back and the sides being circularly joined, and each had four arms and as many legs; two faces fixed upon a round neck, exactly like each other; one head between the two faces; four ears, and two organs of generation; and everything else as from such proportions it is easy to conjecture. Man walked upright as now, in whatever direction he pleased; and when he wished to go fast he made use of all his eight limbs, and proceeded in a rapid motion by rolling circularly round, – like tumblers, who, with their legs in the air, tumble round and round. We account for the production of three sexes by supposing that, at the beginning, the male was produced from the Sun, the female from the Earth; and that sex which participated in both sexes, from the Moon, by reason of the androgynous nature of the Moon. They were round, and their mode of proceeding was round, from the similarity which must needs subsist between them and their parent.

'They were strong also, and had aspiring thoughts. They it was who levied war against the Gods; and what Homer writes concerning Ephialtus and Otus, that they sought to ascend heaven and dethrone the Gods, in reality relates to this primitive people. Jupiter and the other Gods debated what was to be done in this emergency. For neither could they prevail on themselves to destroy them, as they had the Giants, with thunder, so that the race should be abolished; for in that case they would be deprived of the honours of the sacrifices which they were in the custom of receiving from them; nor could they permit a continuance of their insolence and impiety. Jupiter, with some difficulty having devised a scheme, at length spoke. "I think," said he, "I have contrived a method by which we may, by rendering the human race more feeble, quell the insolence which they exercise, without proceeding to their utter destruction. I will cut each of them in half; and so they will at once be weaker and more useful on account of their numbers. They shall walk upright on two legs. If they show any more insolence, and will not keep quiet, I will cut them up in half again, so they shall go about hopping on one leg."

'So saying, he cut human beings in half, as people cut eggs before they salt them, or as I have seen eggs cut with hairs. He ordered Apollo to take each one as he cut him, and turn his face and half his neck towards the operation, so that by contemplating it he might become more cautious and humble; and then to cure him, Apollo turned the face round, and drawing the skin upon what we now call the belly, like a contracted pouch, and leaving one opening, that which is called the navel, tied it in the middle. He then smoothed many other wrinkles, and moulded the breast with much such an instrument as the leather-cutters use to smooth the skins upon the block. He left only a few wrinkles in the belly, near the navel, to serve as a record of its former adventure. Immediately after this division, as each desired to possess the other half of himself, these divided people threw their arms around and embraced each other, seeking to grow together; and from this resolution to do nothing without the other half, they died of hunger and weakness: when one half died and the other was left alive, that which was thus left sought the other and folded it to its bosom; whether that half were an entire woman (for we now call it a woman) or a man; and thus they perished. But Jupiter, pitying them, thought of another contrivance, and placed the parts of generation before. Since formerly when these parts were exposed they produced their kind not by the assistance of each other, but like grasshoppers, by engendering upon the earth. In this manner is generation now produced, by the union of male and female; so that from the embrace of a man and woman the race is propagated, but from those of the same sex no such consequence ensues.

'From this period, mutual Love has naturally existed in human beings; that reconciler and bond of union of their original nature, which seeks to make two, one, and to heal the divided nature of man. Every one of us is thus the half of what may be properly termed a man, and like a *psetta** cut in two, is the imperfect portion of an entire whole, perpetually necessitated to seek the half belonging to him. Those who are a section of what was formerly one man and woman, are lovers of the female sex, and most of the adulterers, and those women who fall in love with men and intrigue with them, belong to this species. Those women who are a section of what in its unity contained two women, are not much attracted by the male sex, but have their inclinations principally engaged by their own. And the *Hetairistriae*† belong to this division. Those who are a section of what in the beginning was entirely male seek the society of males; and before they arrive at manhood, such being portions of what was masculine, are delighted with the intercourse and familiarity of men. These are the youths who, being of a more manly nature, promise the fairest harvest of future excellence. Some attach to them the reproach of libertinism and immodesty, but without justice; for they do not seek an intercourse with men from any immodesty but from the impulses of a generous, aspiring and manly nature. A great proof of which is that such alone ever attain to political power. When they arrive at manhood they still only associate with those of their own sex; and they never engage in marriage and the propa-

---

* A kind of flat fish, like a turbot, which can be divided down the spine into two symmetrical halves. [*ed.*]

† Female homosexuals. [*ed.*]

gation of the species from sensual desire but only in obedience to the laws. It would be sufficient to them if they lived for ever unmarried in the mutual society of their equals.

'Such as I have described is ever an affectionate lover and a faithful friend, delighting in that which is in conformity with his own nature. Whenever, therefore, any such as I have described are impetuously struck, through the sentiment of their former union, with love and desire and the want of community, they are ever unwilling to be divided even for a moment. These are they who devote their whole lives to each other, with a vain and inexpressible longing to obtain from each other something they know not what; for it is not merely the sensual delights of their intercourse for the sake of which they dedicate themselves to each other with such serious affection; but the soul of each manifestly thirsts for, from the other, something which there are no words to describe, and divines that which it seeks, and traces obscurely the footsteps of its obscure desire. If Vulcan should stand over the couch of these persons thus affected as they were reclining together, with his tools, and should say to them, "My good people, what is it that you want with one another?" And if, while they were hesitating what to answer, he should proceed to ask, "Do you not desire the closest union and singleness to exist between you, so that you may never be divided night or day? If so, I will melt you together, and make you grow into one, so that both in life and death ye may be undivided. Consider, is this what you desire? Will it content you if you become that which I propose?" We all know that no one would refuse such an offer, but would at once feel that this was what he had ever sought; and intimately to mix and melt and to be melted together with his beloved, so that one should be made out of two.

'The cause of this desire is, that according to our original nature, we were once entire. The desire and the pursuit of integrity and union is that which we all love. First, as I said, we were entire, but now we have been divided through our own wickedness, as the Arcadians by the Lacedaemonians. There is reason to fear, if we are guilty of any additional impiety towards the Gods, that we may be cut in two again, and may go about like those figures painted on the columns, divided through the middle of our nostrils, as thin as *lispae*.* On which account every man ought to be exhorted to pay due reverence to the Gods, that we may escape so severe a punishment, and obtain those things which Love, our general and commander, incites us to desire; against whom let none rebel by exciting the hatred of the Gods. For if we continue on good terms with them, we may discover and possess those lost and concealed objects of our love; a good-fortune which now befalls to few. Nor let Eryximachus take up that expression as if I alluded to Pausanias and Agathon, for probably they who are manly by nature, are to be ranked among those fortunate few.

'I assert, then, that the happiness of all, both men and women, consists singly in the fulfilment of their Love, and in that possession of its objects by which we are in some degree restored to our ancient nature. If this be the completion of felicity, that must necessarily approach nearest to it, in which we obtain the possession and society of those whose natures most intimately accord with our own. And if we would celebrate any God as the author of this benefit, we should justly celebrate Love with hymns of joy; who, in our present condition, brings good assistance in our necessity, and affords great hopes, if we persevere in piety towards the Gods, that he will restore us to our original state, and confer on us the complete happiness alone suited to our nature.

'Such, Eryximachus, is my discourse on the subject of Love; different indeed from yours, which I nevertheless entreat you not to turn into ridicule, that we may not interrupt what each has separately to deliver on the subject.'

'I will refrain at present,' said Eryximachus, 'for your discourse delighted me. And if I did not know that Socrates and Agathon were profoundly versed in the science of love affairs, I should fear that they had nothing new to say, after so many and such various imaginations. As it is, I confide in the

---

* 'Dice cut in two by friends, each of whom kept half as a tally.' – Liddell & Scott, *Greek Lexicon*. Obviously as a pledge of love. [ed.]

fertility of their geniuses.' – 'Your part of the contest, at least, was strenuously fought, Eryximachus,' said Socrates, 'but if you had been in the situation in which I am, or rather shall be, after the discourse of Agathon, like me, you would then have reason to fear, and be reduced to your wits' end.' – 'Socrates,' said Agathon, 'wishes to confuse me with the enchantments of his wit, sufficiently confused already with the expectation I see in the assembly in favour of my discourse.' – 'I must have lost my memory, Agathon,' replied Socrates, 'if I imagined that you could be disturbed by a few private persons, after having witnessed your firmness and courage in ascending the rostrum with the actors, and in calmly reciting your compositions in the presence of so great an assembly as that which decreed you the prize of tragedy.' – 'What then, Socrates,' retorted Agathon, 'do you think me so full of the theatre as to be ignorant that the judgement of a few wise is more awful than that of a multitude of others, to one who rightly balances the value of their suffrages?' – 'I should judge ill indeed, Agathon,' answered Socrates, 'in thinking you capable of any rude and unrefined conception, for I well know that if you meet with any whom you consider wise, you esteem such alone of more value than all others. But we are far from being entitled to this distinction, for we were also of that assembly, and to be numbered among the rest. But should you meet with any who are really wise, you would be careful to say nothing in their presence which you thought they would not approve – is it not so?' – 'Certainly,' replied Agathon. – 'You would not then exercise the same caution in the presence of the multitude in which they were included?' – 'My dear Agathon,' said Phaedrus, interrupting him, 'if you answer all the questions of Socrates, they will never have an end; he will urge them without conscience so long as he can get any person, especially one who is so beautiful, to dispute with him. I own it delights me to hear Socrates discuss; but at present, I must see that Love is not defrauded of the praise, which it is my province to exact from each of you. Pay the God his due, and then reason between yourselves if you will.'

'Your admonition is just, Phaedrus,' replied Agathon, 'nor

need any reasoning I hold with Socrates impede me; we shall find many future opportunities for discussion. I will begin my discourse then, first having defined what ought to be the subject of it. All who have already spoken seem to me not so much to have praised Love, as to have felicitated mankind on the many advantages of which that deity is the cause; what he is, the author of these great benefits, none have yet declared. There is one mode alone of celebration which would comprehend the whole topic, namely, first to declare what are those benefits, and then what he is who is the author of those benefits, which are the subject of our discourse. Love ought first to be praised, and then his gifts declared. I assert, then, that although all the Gods are immortally happy, Love, if I dare trust my voice to express so awful a truth, is the happiest, and most excellent, and the most beautiful. That he is the most beautiful is evident; first, O Phaedrus, from this circumstance, that he is the youngest of the Gods; and, secondly, from his fleetness, and his repugnance to all that is old; for he escapes with the swiftness of wings from old age; a thing in itself sufficiently swift, since it overtakes us sooner than there is need; and which Love, who delights in the intercourse of the young, hates, and in no manner can be induced to enter into community with. The ancient proverb, which says that like is attracted by like, applies to the attributes of Love. I concede many things to you, O Phaedrus, but this I do not concede, that Love is more ancient than Saturn and Iapetus. I assert that he is not only the youngest of the Gods, but invested with everlasting youth. Those ancient deeds among the Gods recorded by Hesiod and Parmenides, if their relations are to be considered as true, were produced not by Love, but by Necessity. For if Love had been then in Heaven, those violent and sanguinary crimes never would have taken place; but there would ever have subsisted that affection and peace, in which the Gods now live, under the influence of Love.

'He is young, therefore, and being young is tender and soft. There were need of some poet like Homer to celebrate the delicacy and tenderness of Love. For Homer says, that the Goddess Calamity is delicate, and that her feet are tender.

"Her feet are soft," he says, "for she treads not upon the ground, but makes her path upon the heads of men." He gives as an evidence of her tenderness, that she walks not upon that which is hard, but that which is soft. The same evidence is sufficient to make manifest the tenderness of Love. For Love walks not upon the earth, nor over the heads of men, which are not indeed very soft; but he dwells within, and treads on the softest of existing things, having established his habitation within the souls and inmost nature of Gods and men; not indeed in all souls – for wherever he chances to find a hard and rugged disposition, there he will not inhabit, but only where it is most soft and tender. Of needs must he be the most delicate of all things, who touches lightly with his feet only the softest parts of those things which are the softest of all.

'He is then the youngest and the most delicate of all divinities; and in addition to this, he is, as it were, the most moist and liquid. For if he were otherwise, he could not, as he does, fold himself around everything, and secretly flow out and into every soul. His loveliness, that which Love possesses far beyond all other things, is a manifestation of the liquid and flowing symmetry of his form; for between deformity and Love there is eternal contrast and repugnance. His life is spent among flowers, and this accounts for the immortal fairness of his skin; for the winged Love rests not in his flight on any form, or within any soul the flower of whose loveliness is faded, but there remains most willingly where is the odour and radiance of blossoms, yet unwithered. Concerning the beauty of the God, let this be sufficient, though many things must remain unsaid. Let us next consider the virtue and power of Love.

'What is most admirable in Love is, that he neither inflicts nor endures injury in his relations either with Gods or men. Nor if he suffers any thing does he suffer it through violence, nor doing anything does he act it with violence, for Love is never even touched with violence. Every one willingly administers every thing to Love; and that which every one voluntarily concedes to another, the laws, which are the kings of the republic, decree that it is just for him to possess. In addition to justice, Love participates in the highest temperance; for if temperance is defined to be the being superior to and holding under dominion pleasures and desires; then Love, than whom no pleasure is more powerful, and who is thus more powerful than all persuasions and delights, must be excellently temperate. In power and valour Mars cannot contend with Love: the love of Venus possesses Mars; the possessor is always superior to the possessed, and he who subdues the most powerful must of necessity be the most powerful of all.

'The justice and temperance and valour of the God have been thus declared; – there remains to exhibit his wisdom. And first, that, like Eryximachus, I may honour my own profession, the God is a wise poet; so wise that he can even make a poet one who was not before: for every one, even if before he were ever so undisciplined, becomes a poet as soon as he is touched by Love; a sufficient proof that Love is a great poet, and well skilled in that science according to the discipline of music. For what any one possesses not, or knows not, that can he neither give nor teach another. And who will deny that the divine poetry, by which all living things are produced upon the earth, is not harmonized by the wisdom of Love? Is it not evident that Love was the author of all the arts of life with which we are acquainted, and that he whose teacher has been Love, becomes eminent and illustrious, whilst he who knows not Love, remains forever unregarded and obscure? Apollo invented medicine, and divination, and archery, under the guidance of desire and Love; so that Apollo was the disciple of Love. Through him the Muses discovered the arts of literature, and Vulcan that of moulding brass, and Minerva the loom, and Jupiter the mystery of the dominion which he now exercises over Gods and men. So were the Gods taught and disciplined by the love of that which is beautiful; for there is no love towards deformity.

'At the origin of things, as I have before said, many fearful deeds are reported to have been done among the Gods, on account of the dominion of Necessity. But so soon as this deity sprang forth from the desire which forever tends in

Bacchus and Ampelus

Laocoön

Niobe

Left: Venus
Anadyomone

Below: Sleeping
Hermaphrodite

Right: Percy
Bysshe Shelley,
1819

Below: Casa
Magni, Lerici,
from a photo-
graph taken in
the 1880s

the Universe towards that which is lovely, then all blessings descended upon all living things, human and divine. Love seems to me, O Phaedrus, a divinity the most beautiful and the best of all, and the author to all others of the excellencies with which his own nature is endowed. Nor can I restrain the poetic enthusiasm which takes possession of my discourse, and bids me declare that Love is the divinity who creates peace among men, and calm upon the sea, the windless silence of storms, repose and sleep in sadness. Love divests us of all alienation from each other, and fills our vacant hearts with overflowing sympathy; he gathers us together in such social meetings as we now delight to celebrate, our guardian and our guide in dances, and sacrifices, and feasts. Yes, Love who showers benignity upon the world, and before whose presence all harsh passions flee and perish; the author of all soft affections; the destroyer of all ungentle thoughts; merciful, mild; the object of the admiration of the wise, and the delight of Gods; possessed by the fortunate, and desired by the unhappy, therefore unhappy because they possess him not; the father of grace, and delicacy, and gentleness, and delight, and persuasion, and desire; the cherisher of all that is good, the abolisher of all evil; our most excellent pilot, defence, saviour and guardian in labour and in fear, in desire and in reason; the ornament and governor of all things human and divine; the best, the loveliest; in whose footsteps everyone ought to follow, celebrating him excellently in song, and bearing each his part in that divinest harmony which Love sings to all things which live and are, soothing the troubled minds of Gods and men. This, O Phaedrus, is what I have to offer in praise of the Divinity; partly composed, indeed, of thoughtless and playful fancies, and partly of such serious ones, as I could well command.'

No sooner had Agathon ceased, than a loud murmur of applause arose from all present; so becomingly had the fair youth spoken, both in praise of the God, and in extenuation of himself. Then Socrates, addressing Eryximachus, said, 'Was not my fear reasonable, son of Acumenus? Did I not divine what has, in fact, happened, – that Agathon's discourse would be so wonderfully beautiful, as to pre-occupy all interest in what I should say?' – 'You, indeed, divined well so far, O Socrates,' said Eryximachus, 'that Agathon would speak eloquently, but not that, therefore, you would be reduced to any difficulty.' – 'How, my good friend, can I or any one else be otherwise than reduced to difficulty, who speak after a discourse so various and so eloquent, and which otherwise had been sufficiently wonderful, if, at the conclusion, the splendour of the sentences, and the choice selection of the expressions, had not struck all the hearers with astonishment; so that I, who well know that I can never say anything nearly so beautiful as this, would, if there had been any escape, have run away for shame. The story of Gorgias came into my mind, and I was afraid lest in reality I should suffer what Homer describes; and lest Agathon, scaring my discourse with the head of the eloquent Gorgias, should turn me to stone for speechlessness. I immediately perceived how ridiculously I had engaged myself with you to assume a part in rendering praise to Love, and had boasted that I was well skilled in amatory matters, being so ignorant of the manner in which it is becoming to render him honour, as I now perceive myself to be. I, in my simplicity, imagined that the truth ought to be spoken concerning each of the topics of our praise, and that it would be sufficient, choosing those which are the most honourable to the God, to place them in as luminous an arrangement as we could. I had, therefore, great hopes that I should speak satisfactorily, being well aware that I was acquainted with the true foundations of the praise which we have engaged to render. But since, as it appears, that our purpose has been, not to render Love his due honour, but to accumulate the most beautiful and the greatest attributes of his divinity, whether they in truth belong to it or not, and that the proposed question is not how Love ought to be praised, but how we should praise him most eloquently, my attempt must of necessity fail. It is on this account, I imagine, that in your discourses you have attributed everything to Love, and have described him to be the author of such and so great effects as, to those who are ignorant of his true nature, may exhibit him as the most beautiful and the best of all things. Not, indeed, to those who know the truth. Such praise has a splendid and imposing effect, but as I am unacquainted with the art of rendering it, my mind, which could not foresee what would be required of me, absolves me from that which my tongue promised. Farewell, then, for such praise I can never render.

'But if you desire, I will speak what I feel to be true; and that I may not expose myself to ridicule, I entreat you to consider that I speak without entering into competition with those who have preceded me. Consider, then, Phaedrus, whether you will exact from me such a discourse, containing the mere truth with respect to Love, and composed of such unpremeditated expressions as may chance to offer themselves to my mind.' – Phaedrus and the rest bade him speak in the manner which he judged most befitting. – 'Permit me, then, O Phaedrus, to ask Agathon a few questions, so that, confirmed by his agreement with me, I may proceed.' – 'Willingly,' replied Phaedrus, 'ask.' – Then Socrates thus began:–

'I applaud, dear Agathon, the beginning of your discourse, where you say, we ought first to define and declare what Love is, and then his works. This rule I particularly approve. But, come, since you have given us a discourse of such beauty and majesty concerning Love, you are able, I doubt not, to explain this question, whether Love is the Love of something or nothing? I do not ask you of what parents Love is; for the enquiry, of whether Love is the love of any father or mother, would be sufficiently ridiculous. But if I were asking you to describe that which a father is, I should ask, not whether a father was the love of any one, but whether a father was the father of any one or not; you would undoubtedly reply, that a father was the father of a son or daughter; would you not?' – 'Assuredly.' – 'You would define a mother in the same manner?' – 'Without doubt.' – 'Yet bear with me, and answer a few more questions, for I would learn from you that which I wish to know. If I should enquire, in addition, is not a brother, through the very nature of his relation, the brother of some one?' – 'Certainly.' – 'Of a brother or sister is he not?' – 'Without question.' – 'Try to explain to me then the nature of Love; Love is the love of something or nothing?' – 'Of something, certainly.'

'Observe and remember this concession. Tell me yet farther, whether Love desires that of which it is the Love or not?' – 'It desires it, assuredly.' – 'Whether possessing that which it desires and loves, or not possessing it, does it desire and love?' – 'Not possessing, I should imagine.' – 'Observe now, whether it does not appear, that, of necessity, desire desires that which it wants and does not possess, and no longer desires that which it no longer wants: this appears to me, Agathon, of necessity to be; how does it appear to you?' – 'It appears so to me also.' – 'Would any one who was already illustrious, desire to be illustrious; would any one already strong, desire to be strong? From what has already been conceded, it follows that he would not. If any one already strong, should desire to be strong; or any one already swift, should desire to be swift; or any one already healthy, should desire to be healthy, it must be concluded that they still desired the advantages of what they already seemed possessed. To destroy the foundation of this error, observe, Agathon, that each of these persons must possess the several advantages in question, at the moment present to our thoughts, whether he will or not. And, now, is it possible that those advantages should be at that time the objects of his desire? For, if any one should say, being in health, "I desire to be in health"; being rich, "I desire to be rich, and thus still desire those things which I already possess," we might say to him, "You, my friend, possess health, and strength, and riches; you do not desire to possess now, but to continue to possess them in the future; for, whether you will or not, they now belong to you. Consider then, whether, when you say that you desire things present to you, and in your own possession, you say anything else than that you desire the advantages to be for the future also in your possession." What else could he reply?' – 'Nothing, indeed.' – 'Is not Love, then, the love of that which is not within its reach, and which cannot hold in security, for the future, those things of which it obtains a present and transitory possession?' – 'Evidently.' – 'Love, therefore, and every thing else that desires anything, desires that which is absent and beyond his reach, that which it has not, that which is not itself, that which it wants; such are the things of which there are desire and love.' – 'Assuredly.'

'Come,' said Socrates, 'let us review your concessions. Is Love anything else than the love first of something; and, secondly, of those things of which it has need?' – 'Nothing.' – 'Now, remember of those things you said in your discourse, that Love was the love – if you wish I will remind you. I think you said something of this kind, that all the affairs of the Gods were admirably disposed through the love of the things which are beautiful; for there was no love of things deformed; did you not say so?' – 'I confess that I did.' – 'You said what was most likely to be true, my friend; and if the matter be so, the love of beauty must be one thing, and the love of deformity another.' – 'Certainly.' – 'It is conceded, then, that Love loves that which he wants but possesses not?' – 'Yes, certainly.' – 'But Love wants and does not possess beauty?' – 'Indeed it must necessarily follow.' – 'What, then! call you that beautiful which has need of beauty and possesses not?' – 'Assuredly no.' – 'Do you still assert, then, that Love is beautiful, if all that we have said be true?' – 'Indeed, Socrates,' said Agathon, 'I am in danger of being convicted of ignorance, with respect to all that I then spoke.' – 'You spoke most eloquently, my dear Agathon; but bear with my questions yet a moment. You admit that things which are good are also beautiful?' – 'No doubt.' – 'If Love, then, be in want of beautiful things, and things which are good are beautiful, he must be in want of things which are good?' – 'I cannot refute your arguments, Socrates.' – 'You cannot refute truth, my dear Agathon: to refute Socrates is nothing difficult.

'But I will dismiss these questionings. At present let me endeavour, to the best of my power, to repeat to you, on the basis of the points which have been agreed upon between me and Agathon, a discourse concerning Love, which I formerly heard from the prophetess Diotima, who was profoundly skilled in this and many other doctrines, and who, ten years before the pestilence, procured to the Athenians, through their sacrifices, a delay of the disease; for it was she who taught me the science of things relating to Love.

'As you well remarked, Agathon, we ought to declare who and what is Love, and then his works. It is easiest to relate them in the same order, as the foreign prophetess observed when, questioning me, she related them. For I said to her much the same things that Agathon has just said to me – that Love was a great deity, and that he was beautiful; and she refuted me with the same reasons as I have employed to refute Agathon, compelling me to infer that he was neither beautiful or good, as I said – "What then," I objected, "O Diotima, is Love ugly and evil?" – "Good words, I entreat you," said Diotima; "do you think that every thing which is not beautiful, must of necessity be ugly?" – "Certainly." – "And every thing that is not wise, ignorant? Do you not perceive that there is something between ignorance and wisdom?" – "What is that?" "To have a right opinion or conjecture. Observe, that this kind of opinion, for which no reason can be rendered, cannot be called knowledge; for how can that be called knowledge, which is without evidence or reason? Nor ignorance, on the other hand; for how can that be called ignorance which arrives at the persuasion of that which it really is? A right opinion is something between understanding and ignorance." – I confessed that what she alleged was true. – "Do not then say," she continued, "that what is not beautiful is of necessity deformed, nor what is not good is of necessity evil; nor, since you have confessed that Love is neither beautiful or good, infer, therefore, that he is deformed or evil, but rather something intermediate."

'"But," I said, "Love is confessed by all to be a great God." – "Do you mean, when you say all, all those who know, or those who know not, what they say?" – "All collectively." – "And how can that be, Socrates?" said she laughing; "how can he be acknowledged to be a great God, by those who assert that he is not even a God at all?" – "And who are they?" I said. – "You for one, and I for another." – "How can you say that, Diotima?" – "Easily," she replied, "and with truth; for tell me, do you not own that all the Gods are beautiful and happy? or will you presume to maintain that any God is otherwise?" – "By Jupiter, not I!" – "Do you not call those alone happy who possess all things that are beautiful and good?" – "Certainly." – "You have confessed that Love, through his desire for things beautiful and good, possesses not those materials of happiness." – "Indeed such was my concession." – "But how can we conceive a God to be without the possession of what is beautiful and good?" – "In no manner, I confess." – "Observe, then, that you do not consider Love to be a God." – "What then," I said, "is Love a mortal?" – "By no means." – "But what, then?" – "Like those things which I have before instanced, he is neither mortal or immortal, but something intermediate." – "What is that, O Diotima?" – "A great Daemon, Socrates; and every thing daemoniacal holds an intermediate place between what is divine and what is mortal."

' "What is his power and nature?" I enquired. – "He interprets and makes a communication between divine and human things, conveying the prayers and sacrifices of men to the Gods, and communicating the commands and directions concerning the mode of worship most pleasing to them, from Gods to men. He fills up that intermediate space between these two classes of beings, so as to bind together, by his own power, the whole universe of things. Through him subsist all divination, and the science of sacred things as it relates to sacrifices, and expiations, and disenchantments, and prophecy, and magic. The divine nature cannot immediately communicate with what is human, but all that intercourse and converse which is conceded by the Gods to men, both whilst they sleep and when they wake, subsists through the intervention of Love; and he who is wise in the science of this intercourse is supremely happy, and participates in the daemoniacal nature; whilst he who is wise in any other science or art, remains a mere ordinary slave. These daemons are, indeed, many and various, and one of them is Love."

' "Who are the parents of Love?" I enquired. – "The history of what you ask," replied Diotima, "is somewhat long; nevertheless I will explain it to you. On the birth of Venus the Gods celebrated a great feast, and among them came Plenty, the son of Metis. After supper, Poverty, observing the profusion, came to beg, and stood beside the door.

Plenty being drunk with nectar, for wine was not yet invented, went out into Jupiter's garden, and fell into a deep sleep. Poverty wishing to have a child by Plenty, on account of her low estate, lay down by him, and from his embraces conceived Love. Love is, therefore, the follower and servant of Venus, because he was conceived at her birth, and because by nature he is a lover of all that is beautiful, and Venus was beautiful. And since Love is the child of Poverty and Plenty, his nature and fortune participates in that of his parents. He is for ever poor, and so far from being delicate and beautiful, as mankind imagine, he is squalid and withered; he flies low along the ground, and is homeless and unsandalled; he sleeps without covering before the doors, and in the unsheltered streets; possessing thus far his mother's nature, that he is ever the companion of Want. But, inasmuch as he participates in that of his father, he is for ever scheming to obtain things which are good and beautiful; he is fearless, vehement, and strong; a dreadful hunter, for ever weaving some new contrivance; exceedingly cautious and prudent, and full of resources; he is also, during his whole existence, a philosopher, a powerful enchanter, a wizard, and a subtle sophist. And, as his nature is neither mortal nor immortal, on the same day when he is fortunate and successful, he will at one time flourish, and then die away, and then, according to his father's nature, again revive. All that he acquires perpetually flows away from him, so that Love is never either rich or poor, and holding for ever an intermediate state between ignorance and wisdom. The case stands thus: – no God philosophizes or desires to become wise, for he is wise; nor, if there exist any other being who is wise, does he philosophize. Nor do the ignorant philosophize, for they desire not to become wise; for this is the evil of ignorance, that he who has neither intelligence, nor virtue, nor delicacy of sentiment, imagines that he possesses all those things sufficiently. He seeks not, therefore, that possession of whose want they are not aware." – "Who, then, O Diotima," I enquired, "are philosophers, if they are neither the ignorant nor the wise?" – "It is evident, even to a child, that they are those intermediate persons, among whom is Love. For Wisdom is one of the most beautiful of all things; Love is that which thirsts for the beautiful, so that Love is of necessity a philosopher, philosophy being an intermediate state between ignorance and wisdom. His parentage accounts for his condition, being the child of a wise and well-provided father, and of a mother both ignorant and poor.

'"Such is the daemoniacal nature, my dear Socrates; nor do I wonder at your error concerning Love, for you thought, as I conjecture from what you say, that Love was not the lover but the beloved, and thence, well concluded that he must be supremely beautiful; for that which is the object of Love must indeed be fair, and delicate, and perfect, and most happy; but Love inherits, as I have declared, a totally opposite nature." – "Your words have persuasion in them, O stranger," I said; "be it as you say. But this Love, what advantage does he afford to men?" – "I will proceed to explain it to you, Socrates. Love being such and so produced as I have described, is, indeed, as you say, the love of things which are beautiful. But if any one should ask us, saying: O Socrates and Diotima, why is Love the love of beautiful things? Or, in plainer words, what does the lover of that which is beautiful, love in the object of his love, and seek from it?" – "He seeks," I said, interrupting her, "the property and possession of it." – "But that," she replied, "might still be met with another question, What has he, who possesses that which is beautiful?" – "Indeed, I cannot immediately reply." – "But if, changing the beautiful for good, any one should enquire, – I ask, O Socrates, what is that which he who loves that which is good, loves in the object of his love?" – "To be in his possession," I replied. – "And what has he, who has the possession of good?" – "This question is of easier solution: he is happy." – "Those who are happy, then, are happy through the possession; and it is useless to enquire what he desires, who desires to be happy; the question seems to have a complete reply. But do you think that this wish and this love are common to all men, and that all desire, that that which is good should be for ever present to them?" – "Certainly, common to all." – "Why do we not say then, Socrates, that every one loves? if, indeed, all love perpetually the same thing? But we say that some love, and some do not." – "Indeed I wonder why it is so." – "Wonder not," said Diotima, "for we select a particular species of love, and apply to it distinctively the appellation of that which is universal." –

'"Give me an example of such a select application." – "Poetry; which is a general name signifying every cause whereby anything proceeds from that which is not, into that which is; so that the exercise of every inventive art is poetry, and all such artists poets. Yet they are not called poets, but distinguished by other names; and one portion or species of poetry, that which has relation to music and rhythm, is divided from all others, and known by the name belonging to all. For this is alone properly called poetry, and those who exercise the art of this species of poetry, poets. So, with respect to Love. Love is indeed universally all that earnest desire for the possession of happiness and that which is good; the greatest and the subtlest love, and which inhabits the heart of every human being; but those who seek this object through the acquirement of wealth, or the exercise of the gymnastic arts, or philosophy, are not said to love, nor are called lovers; one species alone is called Love, and those alone are said to be lovers, and to love, who seek the attainment of the universal desire through one species of Love, which is peculiarly distinguished by the name belonging to the whole. It is asserted by some, that they love, who are seeking the lost half of their divided being. But I assert, that Love is neither the love of the half or of the whole, unless, my friend, it meets with that which is good; since men willingly cut off their own hands and feet, if they think that they are the cause of evil to them. Nor do they cherish and embrace that which may belong to themselves, merely because it is their own; unless, indeed, any one should choose to say, that that which is good is attached to his own nature and is his own, whilst that which is evil is foreign and accidental; but love nothing but that which is good. Does it not appear so to you?" – "Assuredly." – "Can we then simply affirm that men love that which is good?" – "Without doubt." – "What, then, must we not add, that, in addition to loving that which is good, they love that it should be present to themselves?" – "Indeed that must be added." – "And not merely that it should be present, but that it should ever be present?" – "This also must be added."

'"Love, then, is collectively the desire in men that good should be for ever present to them." – "Most true." – "Since this is the general definition of Love, can you explain in what mode of attaining its object, and in what species of actions, does Love peculiarly consist?" – "If I knew what you ask, O Diotima, I should not have so much wondered at your wisdom, or have sought you out for the purpose of deriving improvement from your instructions." – "I will tell you," then she replied: "Love is the desire of generation in the beautiful, both with relation to the body and the soul." – "I must be a diviner to comprehend what you say, for, being such as I am, I confess that I do not understand it." – "But I will explain it more clearly. The bodies and the souls of all human beings are alike pregnant with their future progeny, and when we arrive at a certain age, our nature impels us to bring forth and propagate. This nature is unable to produce in that which is deformed, but it can produce in that which is beautiful. The intercourse of the male and female in generation, a divine work, through pregnancy and production, is, as it were, something immortal in mortality. These things cannot take place in that which is incongruous; for that which is deformed is incongruous, but that which is beautiful is congruous with what is immortal and divine. Beauty is, therefore, the Fate, and the Juno Lucina to generation. Wherefore, whenever that which is pregnant with the generative principle, approaches that which is beautiful, it becomes transported with delight, and is poured forth in overflowing pleasure, and propagates. But when it approaches that which is deformed, it is contracted and sad, it is repelled and checked and does not produce, but retains unwillingly that with which it is pregnant. Wherefore, to one pregnant, and, as it were, already bursting with the load of his desire, the impulse towards that which is beautiful is intense, on account of the great pain of retaining that which he has conceived. Love, then, O Socrates, is not as you imagine the love of the beautiful." – "What, then?" – "Of generation and production in the beautiful." – "Why then of generation?" – "Generation is something eternal and immortal in mortality. It necessarily, from what has been confessed, follows, that we must desire immortality together with what is good, since Love is the desire that good be for ever present to us. Of necessity Love must also be the desire of immortality."

'Diotima taught me all this doctrine in the discourse we had together concerning Love; and in addition, she enquired, "What do you think, Socrates, is the cause of this love and desire? Do you not perceive how all animals, both those of the earth and of the air, are affected when they desire the propagation of their species, affected even to weakness and disease by the impulse of their love; first, longing to be mixed with each other, and then seeking nourishment for their off-spring, so that the feeblest are ready to contend with the strongest in obedience to this law, and to die for the sake of their young, or to waste away with hunger, and do or suffer anything so that they may not want nourishment. It might be said that human beings do these things through reason, but can you explain why other animals are thus affected through love?" I confessed that I did not know. – "Do you imagine yourself," said she, "to be skilful in the science of Love, if you are ignorant of these things?" – "As I said before, O Diotima, I come to you, well knowing how much I am in need of a teacher. But explain to me, I entreat you, the cause of these things, and of the other things relating to Love." – "If," said Diotima, "you believe that Love is of the same nature as we have mutually agreed upon, wonder not that such are its effects. For the mortal nature seeks, so far as it is able, to become deathless and eternal. But it can only accomplish this desire by generation, which for ever leaves another new in place of the old. For, although each human being be severally said to live, and be the same from youth to old age, yet, that which is called the same, never contains within itself the same things, but always is becoming new by the loss and change of that which it possessed before; both the hair, and the flesh, and the bones, and the entire body.

'"And not only does this change take place in the body, but also with respect to the soul. Manners, morals, opinions, desires, pleasures, sorrows, fears; none of these ever remain unchanged in the same persons; but some die away, and others are produced. And, what is yet more strange is that not only does some knowledge spring up, and another decay, and that we are never the same with respect to our knowledge, but that each several object of our thoughts suffers the same revolution. That which is called meditation, or the exercise of memory, is the science of the escape or departure of knowledge; for, forgetfulness is the going out of knowledge; and meditation, calling up a new memory in the place of that which has departed, preserves knowledge; so that, tho' for ever displaced and restored, it seems to be the same. In this manner every thing mortal is preserved; not that it is constant and eternal, like that which is divine; but that in the place of what has grown old and is departed, it leaves another new like that which it was itself. By this contrivance, O Socrates, does what is mortal, the body and all other things, partake of immortality; that which is immortal, is immortal in another manner. Wonder not, then, if every thing by nature cherishes that which was produced from itself, for this earnest Love is a tendency towards eternity."

'Having heard this discourse, I was astonished, and asked, "Can these things be true, O wisest Diotima?" And she, like an accomplished sophist, said, "Know well, O Socrates, that if you only regard that love of glory which inspires men, you will wonder at your own unskilfulness in not having discovered all that I now declare. Observe with how vehement a desire they are affected to become illustrious and to prolong their glory into immortal time, to attain which object, far more ardently than for the sake of their children, all men are ready to engage in any dangers, and expend their fortunes, and submit to any labours and incur any death. Do you believe that Alcestis would have died in the place of Admetus, or Achilles for the revenge of Patroclus, or Codrus for the kingdom of his posterity, if they had not believed that the immortal memory of their actions, which we now cherish, would have remained after their death? Far otherwise; all such deeds are done for the sake of ever-living virtue, and this immortal glory which they have obtained; and inasmuch as any one is of an excellent nature, so much the more is he impelled to attain this reward. For they love what is immortal.

' "Those whose bodies alone are pregnant with this principle of immortality are attracted by women, seeking through the production of children what they imagine to be happiness and immortality and an enduring remembrance; but they whose souls are far more pregnant than their bodies, conceive and produce that which is more suitable to the soul. What is suitable to the soul? Intelligence, and every other power and excellence of the mind, of which all poets, and all other artists who are creative and inventive, are the authors. The greatest and most admirable wisdom is that which regulates the government of families and states, and which is called moderation and justice. Whosoever, therefore, from his youth feels his soul pregnant with the conception of these excellencies, is divine; and when due time arrives, desires to bring forth; and wandering about, he seeks the beautiful in which he may propagate what he has conceived; for there is no generation in that which is deformed; he embraces those bodies which are beautiful rather than those which are deformed, in obedience to the principle within him which is ever seeking to perpetuate itself. And if he meets, in conjunction with loveliness of form, a beautiful, generous and gentle soul, he embraces both at once, and immediately undertakes to educate this object of his love, and is inspired with an overflowing persuasion to declare what is virtue, and what he ought to be who would attain to its possession, and what are the duties which it exacts. For, by the intercourse with, and as it were, the very touch of that which is beautiful, he brings forth and produces what he had formerly conceived; and nourishes and educates that which is thus produced together with the object of his love, whose image, whether absent or present, is never divided from his mind. So that those who are thus united are linked by a nobler community and a firmer love, as being the common parents of a lovelier and more enduring progeny than the parents of other children.

And every one who considers what posterity Homer and Hesiod and the other great poets have left behind them, the sources of their own immortal memory and renown, or what children of his soul Lycurgus has appointed to be the guardians, not only of Lacedaemon, but of all Greece; or what an illustrious progeny of laws Solon has produced, and how many admirable achievements, both among the Greeks and Barbarians, men have left as the pledges of that love which subsisted between them and the beautiful, would choose rather to be the parent of such children than those in an human shape. For divine honours have often been rendered to them on account of such children, but on account of those in human shape, never.

'"Your own meditation, O Socrates, might perhaps have initiated you in all these things which I have already taught you on the subject of Love. But those perfect and sublime ends, to which these are only the means, I know not that you would have been competent to discover. I will declare them, therefore, and will render them as intelligible as possible; do you meanwhile strain all your attention to trace the obscure depth of the subject. He who aspires to love rightly, ought from his earliest youth to seek an intercourse with beautiful forms, and first to make a single form the object of his love, and therein to generate intellectual excellencies. He ought, then, to consider that beauty in whatever form it resides is the brother of that beauty which subsists in another form; and if he ought to pursue that which is beautiful in form, it would be absurd to imagine that beauty is not one and the same thing in all forms, and would therefore remit much of his ardent preference towards one, through his perception of the multitude of claims upon his love. In addition, he would consider the beauty which is in souls more excellent than that which is in form. So that one endowed with an admirable soul, even though the flower of his form were withered, would suffice him as the object of his love and care, and the companion with whom he might seek and produce such conclusions as tend to the improvement of youth; so that it might be led to observe the beauty and the conformity which there is in the observation of its duties and the laws, and to esteem little the mere beauty of the outward form. The lover would then conduct his pupil to science, so that he might look upon the loveliness of wisdom; and that contemplating thus the universal beauty, no longer like some servant in love with his fellow would he unworthily and meanly enslave himself to the attractions of one form, nor one subject of discipline or science, but would turn towards the wide ocean of intellectual beauty, and from the sight of the lovely and majestic forms which it contains, would abundantly bring forth his conceptions in philosophy; until, strengthened and confirmed, he should at length steadily contemplate one science, which is the science of this universal beauty.

' "Attempt, I entreat you, to mark what I say with as keen an observation as you can. He who has been disciplined to this point in Love, by contemplating beautiful objects gradually, and in their order, now arriving at the end of all that concerns Love, on a sudden beholds a beauty wonderful in its nature. This it is, O Socrates, for the sake of which all the former labours were endured. It is eternal, unproduced, indestructible; neither subject to increase nor decay: not, like other things, partly beautiful and partly deformed; not at one time beautiful and at another time not; not beautiful in relation to one thing and deformed in relation to another; not here beautiful and there deformed; not beautiful in the estimation of one person and deformed in that of another; nor can this supreme beauty be figured to the imagination like a beautiful face, or beautiful hands, or any portion of the body, nor like any discourse, or any science. Nor does it subsist in any other thing that lives or is, either in earth, or in heaven, or in any other place; but it is eternally uniform and consistent, and monoeidic with itself. All other things are beautiful through a participation of it, with this condition, that although they are subject to production and decay, it never becomes more or less, or endures any change. When any one, ascending from a correct system of Love, begins to contemplate this supreme beauty, he already touches the consummation of his labour. For such as discipline themselves upon this system, or are conducted by another beginning to ascend through these transitory objects which are beautiful, towards that which is beauty itself, proceeding as on steps from the love of one form to that of two, and from that of two, to that of all forms which are beautiful; and from beautiful forms to beautiful habits and institutions, and from institutions to beautiful doctrines; until, from the meditation of many doctrines, they arrive at that which is nothing else than the doctrine of the supreme beauty itself, in the knowledge and contemplation of which at length they repose.

'"Such a life, as this, my dear Socrates," exclaimed the stranger prophetess, "spent in the contemplation of the beautiful, is the life for men to live; which if you chance ever to experience, you will esteem far beyond gold and rich garments, and even those lovely persons whom you and many others now gaze on with astonishment, and are prepared neither to eat or drink so that you may behold and live for ever with these objects of your love! What, then, shall we imagine to be the aspect of the supreme beauty itself, simple, pure, uncontaminated with the intermixture of human flesh and colours, and all other idle and unreal shapes attendant on mortality; the divine, the original, the supreme, the self consistent, the monoeidic beautiful itself? What must be the life of him who dwells with and gazes on that which it becomes us all to seek? Think you not that to him alone is accorded the prerogative of bringing forth, not images and shadows of virtue, for he is in contact not with a shadow but with reality; with virtue itself, in the production and nourishment of which he becomes dear to the Gods, and if such a privilege is conceded to any human being, himself immortal."

'Such, O Phaedrus, and my other friends, was what Diotima said. And being persuaded by her words, I have since occupied myself in attempting to persuade others, that it is not easy to find a better assistant than Love in seeking to communicate immortality to our human natures. Wherefore I exhort every one to honour Love; I hold him in honour, and chiefly exercise myself in amatory matters, and exhort others to do so; and now and ever do I praise the power and excellence of Love, in the best manner that I can. Let this discourse, if it pleases you, Phaedrus, be considered as an encomium of Love; or call it by what other name you will.'

The whole assembly praised his discourse, and Aristophanes was on the point of making some remarks on the allusion made by Socrates to him in a part of his discourse, when suddenly they heard a loud knocking at the door of the vestibule, and a clamour as of revellers, attended by a flute-player. – 'Go, boys,' said Agathon, 'and see who is there: if they are any of our friends, call them in; if not, say that we have already done drinking.' – A minute afterwards, they heard the voice of Alcibiades in the vestibule excessively drunk and roaring out: – 'Where is Agathon? Lead me to Agathon!' – The flute-player, and some of his companions, then led him in, and placed him against the door-post, crowned with a thick crown of ivy and violets, and having a quantity of fillets on his head. – 'My friends,' he cried out, 'hail! I am excessively drunk already, but I'll drink with you, if you will. If not, we will go away after having crowned Agathon, for which purpose I came. I assure you that I could not come yesterday, but I am now here with these fillets round my temples, that from my own head I may crown his head who, with your leave, is the most beautiful and wisest of men. Are you laughing at me because I am drunk? Aye, I know what I say is true, whether you laugh or not. But tell me at once, whether I shall come in, or no. Will you drink with me?'

Agathon and the whole party desired him to come in, and recline among them; so he came in, led by his companions. He then unbound his fillets that he might crown Agathon, and though Socrates was just before his eyes, he did not see him, but sat down by Agathon, between Socrates and him, for Socrates moved out of the way to make room for him. When he sat down, he embraced Agathon and crowned him; and Agathon desired the slaves to untie his sandals, that he might make a third, and recline on the same couch. 'By all means,' said Alcibiades, 'but what third companion have we here?' And at the same time turning round and seeing Socrates, he leaped up and cried out: – 'O Hercules! what have we here? You, Socrates, lying in ambush for me wherever

I go! and meeting me just as you always do, when I least expected to see you! And, now, what are you come here for? Why have you chosen to recline exactly in this place, and not near Aristophanes, or any one else who is, or wishes to be ridiculous, but have contrived to lie down beside the most beautiful person of the whole party?' – 'Agathon,' said Socrates, 'see if you cannot defend me. I declare my love for this man is a bad business: from the moment that I first began to love him I have never been permitted to converse with, or so much as to look on any one who is beautiful. If I do, he is so jealous and suspicious that he does the most extravagant things, and hardly refrains from beating me. I entreat you to prevent him from doing anything of that kind at present. Procure a reconciliation: or, if he perseveres in attempting any violence, I entreat you to defend me, for I am seriously alarmed at the fury of his amatory impulse.' – 'Indeed,' said Alcibiades, 'I will not be reconciled to you; I shall find another opportunity to punish you for this. But now,' said he, addressing Agathon, 'lend me some of those fillets, that I may crown the wonderful head of this fellow, lest I incur the blame, that having crowned you, I neglected to crown him who conquers all men with his discourses, not yesterday alone as you did, but ever.'

Saying this he took the fillets, and having bound the head of Socrates, and again having reclined, said: 'Come, my friends, you seem to be sober enough. You must not flinch, but drink, for that was your agreement with me before I came in. I choose as president, until you have drunk enough – myself. Come, Agathon, if you have got a great goblet, fetch it out. But no matter, that wine-cooler will do; bring it, boy!' And observing that it held more than eight cups, he first drank it off, and then ordered it to be filled for Socrates, and said: – 'Observe, my friends, I cannot invent any scheme against Socrates, for he will drink as much as any one desires him, and not be in the least drunk.' Socrates, after the boy had filled up, drank it off; and Eryximachus said: – 'Shall we then have no conversation or singing over our cups, but drink down stupidly, just as if we were thirsty?' And Alcibiades said: – 'Ah, Eryximachus, I did not see you before;

hail, you excellent son of a wise and excellent father!' – 'Hail to you also,' replied Eryximachus, 'but what shall we do?' – 'Whatever you command, for we ought to submit to your directions; a physician is worth an hundred common men. Command us as you please.' – 'Listen then,' said Eryximachus; 'before you came in, each of us had agreed to deliver as eloquent a discourse as he could in praise of Love, beginning at the right hand; all the rest of us have fulfilled our engagement; you have not spoken, and yet have drunk with us: you ought to bear your part in the discussion; and having done so, command what you please to Socrates, who shall have the privilege of doing so to his right-hand neighbour, and so on to the others.' – 'Indeed, there appears some justice in your proposal, Eryximachus, though it is rather unfair to induce a drunken man to set his discourse in competition with that of those who are sober. And, besides, did Socrates really persuade you that what he just said about me was true, or do you not know that matters are in fact exactly the reverse of his representation? For I seriously believe, that, should I praise in his presence, be he God or man, any other beside himself, he would not keep his hands off me.' – 'Good words I entreat you,' said Socrates – 'I charge you by Neptune,' cried Alcibiades, 'to keep quiet, I assure you that I will praise no one beside yourself in your presence.'

'Do so, then,' said Eryximachus; 'praise Socrates if you please.' – 'What!' said Alcibiades, 'shall I attack him, and punish him before you all?' – 'What have you got into your head now,' said Socrates; 'are you going to expose me to ridicule, and to misrepresent me? Or what are you going to do?' – 'I will only speak the truth; will you permit me on this condition?' – 'I not only permit, but exhort you to say all the truth you know,' replied Socrates. 'I obey you willingly,' said Alcibiades; 'and if I advance anything untrue, do you, if you please, interrupt me, and convict me of misrepresentation, for I would never willingly speak falsely. And bear with me if I do not relate things in their order, but just as I remember them, for it is not easy for a man in my present condition to enumerate systematically all your singularities.

'I will begin the praise of Socrates by comparing him to a certain statue. Perhaps he will think that this statue is introduced for the sake of ridicule, but I assure you that it is necessary for the illustration of truth. I assert, then, that Socrates is exactly like those Silenuses that sit in the sculptors' shops, and which are carved holding flutes or pipes, but which, when divided in two, are found to contain withinside the images of the Gods. I assert that Socrates is like the satyr Marsyas. That your form and appearance are like these Satyrs, I think that even you will not venture to deny; and how like you are to them in all other things, now hear. Are you not scornful and petulant? If you deny this, I will bring witnesses. Are you not a piper, and far more wonderful a one than he? For Marsyas, and whoever now pipes the music that he taught (for that music which is of Heaven is described as being taught by Marsyas) enchants men through the power of the mouth. For if any musician, be he skilful or not, awakens this music, it alone enables him to retain the minds of men, and from the divinity of its nature makes evident those who are in want of the Gods and initiation. You differ only from Marsyas in this circumstance, that you effect without instruments, by mere words, all that he can do. For when we hear Pericles, or any other accomplished orator, deliver a discourse, no one, as it were, cares anything about it. But when any one hears you, or even your words related by another, though ever so rude and unskilful a speaker, be that person a woman, man or child, we are struck and retained, as it were, by the discourse clinging to our mind.

'If I was not afraid that I am a great deal too drunk, I would confirm to you by an oath the strange effects which I assure you I have suffered from his words, and suffer still; for when I hear him speak, my heart leaps up far more than the hearts of those who celebrate the Corybantic mysteries; my tears are poured out as he talks, a thing I have seen happen to many others beside myself. I have heard Pericles and other excellent orators, and have been pleased with their discourses, but I suffered nothing of this kind; nor was my soul ever on those occasions disturbed and filled with self-reproach, as if it were slavishly laid prostrate. But this Marsyas here has often affected me in the way I describe, until the life which I lead seemed hardly worth living. Do not deny it, Socrates; for I well know that if even now I chose to listen to you, I could not resist, but should again suffer the same effects. For, my friends, he forces me to confess that while I myself am still in want of many things, I neglect my own necessities, and attend to those of the Athenians. I stop my ears, therefore, as from the Syrens, and flee away as fast as possible, that I may not sit down beside him and grow old in listening to his talk. For this man has reduced me to feel the sentiment of shame, which I imagine no one would readily believe was in me; he alone inspires me with remorse and awe. For I feel in his presence my incapacity of refuting what he says, or of refusing to do that which he directs; but when I depart from him, the glory which the multitude confers overwhelms me. I escape, therefore, and hide myself from him, and when I see him I am overwhelmed with humiliation, because I have neglected to do what I have confessed to him ought to be done; and often and often have I wished that he were no longer to be seen among men. But if that were to happen, I well know that I should suffer far greater pain; so that where I can turn, or what I can do with this man, I know not. All this have I and many others suffered from the pipings of this satyr.

'And observe how like he is to what I said, and what a wonderful power he possesses. Know that there is not one of you who is aware of the real nature of Socrates; but since I have begun, I will make him plain to you. You observe how passionately Socrates affects the intimacy of those who are beautiful, and how ignorant he professes himself to be; appearances in themselves excessively Silenic. This, my friends, is the external form with which, like one of those sculptured Sileni, he has clothed himself; for if you open him, you will find within admirable temperance and wisdom. For he cares not for mere beauty, but despises more than any one can imagine all external possessions, whether it be beauty or wealth, or glory, or any other thing for which the multitude felicitates the possessor. He esteems these things and us who honour them, as nothing, and lives among men, making all the objects of their admiration the playthings of his irony. But I know not if any one of you have ever seen the divine images which are within, when he has been opened and is serious. I have seen them, and they are so supremely beautiful, so golden, so divine, and wonderful, that every thing which Socrates commands surely ought to be obeyed, even like the voice of a God.

'On our first intimacy I imagined that Socrates was in love with me on account of my beauty, and was determined to seize so favourable an opportunity, by conceding to him all that he required, of learning from him all that he knew: for I imagined that my beauty was something irresistible and extraordinary. As soon as I perceived this I sent away the servant, who was accustomed to be present at our meetings, and remained with him alone: for I will tell you the whole truth, therefore now attend; and do you, Socrates, if I say anything that is false, interrupt and refute me. Well, he and I were now alone together and I thought that he would then say all that a lover is accustomed to say in solitude to his beloved, and was rejoiced. But nothing of this kind passed, and after spending the day with me, and talking just as usual, he went away. After this I invited him to exercise with me in gymnastic exercises, hoping that something might arise out of this; and we were very often stript and wrestled together with no other person present. What is the use of more words? Everything failed; and since I could not succeed thus I resolved having once taken it into hand to assail him with more powerful temptations; and now I have once begun I will tell all.

'I invited him to supper, actually laying plots for him as a lover would for his beloved. At first he would not accept my invitation, at last being persuaded he came and went away immediately after supper. I was shamed that time of what I had undertaken and let him go. But laying my plan a second time, I protracted the conversation after supper far into the night, and when he motioned to depart, I prevailed on him to remain, alleging the lateness of the hour. He composed himself to sleep on the couch next to mine on which he had supped: and no one else slept in the house beside ourselves.

So much as this I could relate without difficulty to any one; but I cannot proceed further without reminding you of the proverb that, wine tells truth, whether with or without youth. I cannot pass over, though I have undertaken to praise Socrates, so proud and scornful a deed. Besides I am like one bitten by a viper, who they say will not tell his misfortune to any, but those who are bitten in the same manner, since they alone knowing what it is, will pardon him for whatever he dares to do or say under the mitigation of his pain. I then, bitten by something more keen and vehement than the keenest of all things by which any one ever was bitten, wounded in my very heart and soul, or whatever else you choose to call it, by the words of philosophy which pierce more sharply than a viper's tooth, when they seize on a fresh and not ungenerous spirit, and instigate it to say or do anything, seeing Phaedrus, and Agathon, and Eryximachus, and Pausanias, and Aristodemus, and Aristophanes, and Socrates himself, and the rest of our companions; for ye are all participators with me in the sacred madness and bacchic enthusiasm of philosophy, am willing that you should hear all. Pardon, I entreat you, what then was done and now is said. Let the servants, or if any other profane and unrefined person is present, close their ears with impenetrable gates.

'Well, my friends, as soon as the attendants had withdrawn and the lamp was extinguished I determined to hesitate no longer but plainly to speak my mind. Touching him, therefore, I said: — "Socrates, are you asleep?" — "Not I," said he. — "Do you know what I have been thinking of?" — "Well, what is it?" — "Why," said I, "I esteem you to be the only lover worthy of me, but I imagine that although you feel such tenderness for me as lovers feel, you are ashamed to confess your sentiments. Being such as I am, I should consider myself indeed unwise if I were not prepared to make every return you can desire to your preference, as I would willingly gratify you, not only in this, but in every thing else that my fortune and connection can command; for it has been my earliest ambition to become as virtuous and accomplished as possible, nor can I conceive any companion or guide more excellent than you to conduct me in the path of its attainment; and not conceding all that such a man as you could desire, I should more dread the reproaches of the wise, than conceding it, the idle clamours of the multitude." – Hearing this, Socrates said ironically and just in his way:– "My dear Alcibiades, if what you say of me be true, and if there be any power in me through which you may become better, you must see methinks some very uncommon beauty in me, very different from that loveliness which is so conspicuous in yourself. If you seek my intercourse for the sake of this, and would exchange your beauty against mine, you design no doubt to gain considerably by me: you would possess that which is truly beautiful instead of the opinion and appearance of beauty, gold instead of molten brass. But my dear friend, observe lest you be deceived in me, and I be indeed nothing. The vision of the understanding then grows keen when the radiance of youth first wanes in the eyes, and yours are yet far from this." – Hearing this I said: "My sentiments are such as I have expressed. I have said nothing that I do not mean. Do you only determine what is best for yourself and me." – "This is well," he replied, "for the future we will consider what is best to be done; both concerning what you propose, and concerning all other things." – After this conversation I believed and hoped that my words had wounded him as with a weapon, so rising from my couch and permitting him to say no more, and casting this garment around us both (for it was winter) I lay the whole night with my arms around this truly divine and wonderful being, upon that very old cloak that he has got on now. I know, Socrates, that you cannot deny what I allege. He despised and contemptuously neglected that beauty which I had thus exposed to his rejection, O Judges, for you shall be judges of the insolence of Socrates: know then, by all the Gods and Goddesses, I swear that I awoke and arose from as unimpassioned an embrace as if I had slept with my father or my elder brother! And after this what think you was the contest of my mind, feeling that I had been thus dishonoured, and yet loving the courage, and temperance and wisdom with which I found this man endowed, so excellently as I had not believed could have fallen to the lot of any human being. So that I could neither persevere in my indignation against, or deprive myself of an intercourse with him, or discover any attraction with which I might entice him to my society. For I knew that he was less vulnerable by money than Ajax by iron, and that resource alone with which I had endeavoured to captivate him, had already failed me. I became the prey of doubt and trouble, and enslaved to this man far more than any other was ever enslaved, I wandered about disconsolately. Such as I have declared was the event of what I attempted.

'Some time after this, we were fellow-soldiers, and had our mess together in the camp before Potidaea. Socrates there overcame not only me, but everyone beside, in endurance of toils: when, as often happens in a campaign, we were reduced to few provisions, there were none who could sustain hunger like Socrates; and when he had plenty, he alone seemed to enjoy our military fare. He never drank much willingly, but when he was compelled, he conquered all even in that to which he was least accustomed; and what is most astonishing, no person ever saw Socrates drunk either then or at any other time. In the depth of winter (and the winters there are excessively rigid), he sustained calmly incredible hardships; and amongst other things, whilst the frost was intolerably severe, and no one went out of their tents, or if they went out, wrapt themselves up carefully, and put fleeces under their feet, and bound their legs with hairy skins, Socrates went out only with the same cloak on that he usually wore, and walked barefoot upon the ice; more easily, indeed, than those who had sandalled themselves so delicately: so that the soldiers thought that he did it to mock their want of fortitude. It would indeed be worth while to commemorate all that this brave man did and endured in that expedition. In one instance he was seen early in the morning, standing in one place in meditation; and as he seemed not to be able to unravel the subject of his thoughts, he still continued to stand as enquiring and discussing within himself, and when noon came, the soldiers observed him, and said to one another – "Socrates has been standing there thinking, ever since the morning."

At last some Ionians came to the spot, and having supped, as it was summer, bringing their blankets, they lay down to sleep in the cool; they observed that Socrates continued to stand there the whole night until morning, and that, when the sun rose, he saluted it with a prayer and departed.

'I ought not to omit what Socrates is in battle. For in that battle after which the generals decreed to me the prize of courage, Socrates alone of all men was the saviour of my life, standing by me when I had fallen and was wounded, and preserving both myself and my arms from the hands of the enemy. On that occasion I entreated the generals to decree the prize, as it was most due, to him. And this, O Socrates, you cannot deny, that while the generals, wishing to conciliate a person of my rank, desired to give me the prize, you were far more earnestly desirous than the generals that this glory should be attributed not to yourself, but me.

'But to see Socrates when our army was defeated and scattered in flight at Delium, was a spectacle worthy to behold. On that occasion I was among the cavalry, and he on foot, heavily armed. After the total rout of our troops, he and Laches retreated together; I came up by chance, and seeing them, bade them be of good cheer, for that I would not leave them. As I was on horseback, and therefore less occupied by a regard of my own situation, I could better observe than at Potidaea the beautiful spectacle exhibited by Socrates on this emergence. How superior was he to Laches in presence of mind and courage! Your representation of him on the stage, O Aristophanes, was not wholly unlike his real self on this occasion, for he walked and darted his regards around with a majestic composure, looking tranquilly both on his friends and enemies; so that it was evident to every one, even from afar, that whoever should venture to attack him would encounter a desperate resistance. He and his companion thus departed in safety; for those who are scattered in flight are pursued and killed, whilst men hesitate to touch those who exhibit such a countenance as that of Socrates even in defeat.

'Many other and most wonderful qualities might well be praised in Socrates; but such as these might singly be attributed to others. But that which is unparalleled in Socrates is that he is unlike, and above comparison with, all other men, whether those who have lived in ancient times, or those who exist now. For it may be conjectured, that Brasidas and many others are such as was Achilles. Pericles deserves comparison with Nestor and Antenor; and other excellent persons of various times may, with probability, be drawn into comparison with each other. But to such a singular man as this, both himself and his discourses are so uncommon, no one, should he seek, would find a parallel among the present or the past generations of mankind; unless they should say that he resembled those with whom I lately compared him, for assuredly, he and his discourses are like nothing but the Sileni and the Satyrs. At first I forgot to make you observe how like his discourses are to those Satyrs when they are opened, for, if any one will listen to the talk of Socrates, it will appear to him at first extremely ridiculous; the phrases and expressions which he employs, fold around his exterior the skin, as it were, of a rude and wanton Satyr. He is always talking about great market-asses, and brass-founders, and leather-cutters, and skin-dressers; and this is his perpetual custom, so that any dull and unobservant person might easily laugh at his discourse. But if any one should see it opened, as it were, and get within the sense of his words, he would then find that they alone of all that enters into the mind of man to utter, had a profound and persuasive meaning, and that they were most divine; and that they presented to the mind innumerable images of every excellence, and that they tended towards objects of the highest moment, or rather towards all, that he who seeks the possession of what is supremely beautiful and good, need regard as essential to the accomplishment of his ambition.

'These are the things, my friends, for which I praise Socrates, as well as those which I complain of in him, for I have mixed up in my discourse the peculiar scorn with which he treated me. Not that I have been the only object of his contempt, but Charmides, the son of Glauco, and Euthydemus, the son of Diocles, are deceived in the same manner, imagining that he was their lover, whilst in fact they vainly pursued him as the object of theirs. As to you, Agathon, take my advice; do not let him cheat you. Be admonished, by my sufferings to take care, and not according to the proverb, like a fool grow wise by your own experience.'

Alcibiades having said this, the whole party burst into laughter at the frankness with which he seemed to confess that he was still in love with Socrates; and Socrates said, 'You seem to be sober enough, Alcibiades, else you would not have made such a circuit of words, only to hide the main design for which you made this long speech, and which, as it were carelessly, you just throw in at the last; now, as if you had not said all this for the mere purpose of dividing me and Agathon? You think that I ought to love you and no one else, and that Agathon ought to be loved by you and no one else. I have found you out; it is evident enough for what design you invented all this Satyrical and Silenic drama. But, my dear Agathon, do not let his device succeed. I entreat you to permit no one to throw discord between us.' – 'No doubt,' said Agathon, 'he sat down between us only that he might divide us; but this shall not assist his scheme, for I will come and recline near you.' – 'Do so,' said Socrates, 'come, there is room for you close under me.' – 'Oh, Jupiter!' exclaimed Alcibiades, 'what I endure from that man! He thinks to subdue me every way; but, at least, I pray you, let Agathon recline between us.' – 'Impossible,' said Socrates, 'you have just praised me; I ought to praise him sitting at my right hand. If Agathon reclines under you, he will not praise me before I praise him. Now, my dear friend, allow the young man to receive what praise I can give him. I have a great desire to pronounce his encomium.' – 'Quick, quick, Alcibiades,' said Agathon, 'I cannot stay here, I must change my place, or Socrates will not praise me.' 'This is just like him,' said Alcibiades, 'when Socrates is present it is impossible to catch hold of any of those who are beautiful. I entreat you to observe how easily he found out a plausible pretext for this beautiful Agathon to come and lie down by him.' – Agathon then arose to take his place near Socrates.

He had no sooner reclined than there came in a number of revellers – for some one who had gone out had left the door open – and took their places on the vacant couches, and everything became full of confusion; and no order being observed, every one was obliged to drink a great quantity of wine. Eryximachus, and Phaedrus, and some others, said Aristodemus, went home to bed; that, for his part, he went to sleep on his couch, and slept long and soundly – the nights were then long – until the cock crew in the morning. When he awoke he found that some were still fast asleep, and others had gone home, and that Aristophanes, Agathon, and Socrates had alone stood it out, and were still drinking out of a great goblet which they passed round and round. Socrates was disputing between them. The beginning of their discussion Aristodemus said that he did not recollect, because he was asleep; but it was terminated by Socrates forcing them to confess, that the same person is able to compose both tragedy and comedy, and that the foundations of the tragic and comic arts were essentially the same. They, rather convicted than convinced, went to sleep. Aristophanes first awoke, and then, it being broad daylight, Agathon. Socrates, having put them to sleep, went away, Aristodemus following him; and coming to the Lyceum he washed himself, as he would have done anywhere else, and after having spent the day there in his accustomed manner, went home in the evening.

5

Italian Discords

Introduction

SHELLEY'S REMAINING FOUR YEARS in Italy never really recaptured the visionary calm of that first golden summer in the Apennines. In his subsequent poetry we glimpse the Platonic heights, but in his personal life we find increasing troubles, complications, and unhappiness. The death of little Clara and Willmouse; Mary's nervous breakdown; the rumbling scandal about Claire; blackmail by his Italian servants; a mysterious baby – adopted or illegitimate – left behind in Naples; increasingly difficult relations with Byron; and finally, in the last months, the death of Allegra in a convent, separated from Claire, and the dangerous miscarriage of Mary's last child: these are some of the salient facts of his domestic existence in Italy, that 'paradise of exiles' as he had called it. The two rather stark extracts in this section, one poetry and one prose, are simply intended to indicate to the reader something of the emotional effect which this continuous turmoil had on Shelley, and the degree to which his views on love were tested, and indeed tormented, in the slow fires of daily living between the ages of twenty-six and twenty-nine.

Though the extracts are separated by more than two years – the poem dates from the late autumn of 1818, the letter was written in August 1821 – they both bear on the same intimate topic: the difficulty Shelley had in sustaining his marriage with Mary, and in keeping their love alive. The poem faces this problem in symbolic and semi-dramatic terms; the letter confronts it at the level of a mundane, but painfully significant, domestic crisis. Both draw to the reader's attention a central truth: that Shelley's attachment to Mary, though the most stable and enduring of all his relationships, was neither exclusive nor particularly happy; that it was, in a certain sense, vitally unhappy, and this paradox possibly tells us something unexpected, and even unpalatable about the creative nature of mature love. Within the marriage, Shelley's stormy relations with Claire were an important dynamic element, and the household in Italy seemed to feed upon a constant atmosphere of actual or potential scandal and excitement, with other women (Elise Foggi, Sophia Stacey, Emilia Viviani, Jane Williams) and also other men (Byron, Trelawny, Edward Williams) frequently on – or over – the verge of being drawn into its emotional maelstrom. More-over even for Mary this situation was a powerful regenerator of passion and creative work, and during this period she com-pleted two further novels, *Mathilda* (1819), a disguised account of her breakdown, and *Valperga* (1822), a wild his-torical romance. Shelley's famous proposition that 'most wretched men/ Are cradled into poetry by wrong,/ They learn in suffering what they teach in song' has a particular application to this stage of their lives together.

The extract from *Julian and Maddalo* is chosen to show the degree of violent feeling, emotional contradiction, and sexual guilt that Shelley was now capable of describing and admit-ting to himself; and more than that, capable of containing within the structure of a semi-dramatic poem. It is the work of an experienced, and to a surprising degree objective man. The poem was largely composed at Venice and Byron's sum-mer villa at Este (where Shelley had taken Claire to visit little Allegra). Commentators now broadly agree that the main characters who appear in the poem can be identified directly: the narrator, Julian, is Shelley; Count Maddalo is of course Byron; the little child at the beginning of the extract is Alle-gra; and the mysterious Madman whom they sail out to visit in the gondola is really Shelley's alter ego (like the *Alastor*-poet), a semi-autobiographic projection of his private griefs. The *persona* of the Madman developed from a verse play Shelley had been trying to write about Tasso, the author of the Renaissance courtly love-epic *The Amadigi* (1560). Tasso had gone mad during an imprisonment in Ferrara. Maddalo's name is also taken from this play. What is far less clear is the identity of the unnamed woman who forms the subject of the Madman's agonized monologue at the centre of the extract.

It was during this 1818 visit to Venice that little Clara died, and several biographers have felt that the Madman's misery reflects Mary's bitter recriminations against Shelley, and her increasing withdrawal from him which – after Willmouse's death in Rome – led to her nervous breakdown. There can be little doubt that Shelley's difficulties with Mary are reflected in a general way by the Madman (Shelley later virtually said as much to Leigh Hunt); but the situation is also more complicated. No mention is in fact made of a dead child as the cause of suffering. Instead, a close reading of the extract will show that the Madman's 'secret grief' concerns errors that he has made in love, unhappiness that he has caused, and intense sexual guilt, which in theory his 'creed should have redeemed (him) from repenting'. The terrible results that these have produced – 'loathèd scorn and outrage unrelenting'; and again, 'the fuel/ Of the mind's hell; hate, scorn, remorse, despair' – have subdued him emotionally, if not intellectually:

> . . . Love sometimes leads astray to misery.
> Yet think not though subdued – and I may well
> Say that I am subdued – that the full Hell
> Within me would infect the untainted breast
> Of sacred nature with its own unrest; . . .
>
> . . . Believe that I am ever still the same
> In creed as in resolve, and what may tame
> My heart, must leave the understanding free,
> Or all would sink in this keen agony – . . .

What makes the Madman's guilt so unbearable is the revulsion and blame which his mysterious lady companion now feels for him, in place of love. But is this lady really to be identified with Mary Shelley? The reader must judge for himself, but my own feeling is that Shelley is deliberately hovering on the borders between poetic fiction and transposed autobiography, and in as far as any specific woman is referred to, it is not one woman, but *several*. The multiple identifications of *Epipsychidion* will later provide an authority for this suggestion. In the broken passages of the monologue (broken by Shelley, not his editor) the different sections have different tones – some horrified, some beseeching, some recriminating – and seem turned towards different women. I would suggest the following very tentative identifications, always allowing for the basic fiction of the whole *persona* of the Madman. The passage beginning 'O thou my spirit's mate . . .' refers fundamentally to Mary, in a mode of appeal which Shelley frequently adopted towards her in other poems. The section beginning 'I must remove/ A veil from my pent mind . . .' goes back in memory to the figure of the drowned Harriet, 'pallid as Death's dedicated bride', whose bridal bed is described as a 'tomb' in a terrible image that Shelley had already used about her in his letter to Hogg ('as if a dead and living body had been linked together in loathsome and horrible communion'). The passage immediately following, 'Nay, was it I that wooed thee . . .', turns back to Mary, now with more open bitterness, and yet still containing the poignant memory of *her* words to him: 'I thought/ That thou wert she who said, "You kiss me not/ Ever, I fear you do not love me now" –'.

The next, and most violent passage, 'That you had never seen me . . .', moves on perhaps to Claire. It is important to realize here that the Madman is again quoting the lady's *words to him*: but hysterical, savage words that one would associate far more with Claire's temperament than Mary's (who we know became withdrawn, icy and depressed in grief), apparently reviling a brief 'moment' of love, and wishing that the Madman had castrated himself – 'torn out/ The nerves of manhood by their bleeding root' – rather than become sexually involved with her, only 'to disunite in horror'. Of course this may all be complete poetic fiction, and certainly it is the most controversial identification. Yet the phrases will later be echoed in *Epipsychidion*, in the 'Comet' passage explicitly associated with Claire; and it has so far escaped scholarly notice that the Madman's comment 'for I heard/ And can forget not' deliberately echoes the close of the 'Constantia' poem to Claire which Shelley hid from Mary: 'Alas! that the torn heart can bleed but not forget.'

These observations are very far from solving the many

enigmas associated with *Julian and Maddalo*, which may be counted as Shelley's darkest and most tortured reflection on love. But it does vividly suggest the growing awareness of the mutual pain and suffering entailed in his two marriages, and the need to endure and accept his responsibilities: to suffer and to learn. Moreover the Madman's soliloquy stands inside the dramatic structure of the poem, carefully placed within the discussion of Julian and Maddalo, and given perspective by their comments. This is not the whole truth about love, Shelley seems to imply, but only what it looks like – what it feels like – when things go wrong, when tragedies strike, when breakdowns occur.

The section closes with Shelley's letter to Mary concerning the Hoppner scandal about Claire. It was written during another visit to Byron, at Ravenna in August 1821, and gives a specific example of the strains which their marriage had to endure. It is curious how Byron's presence often seemed to act as a catalyst in Shelley's affairs: it is almost as if the contact between the two poets instantly created a sort of combustible substance, and all the old amorous desires and discontents began to smoulder and catch fire again.

The biographical intricacies of the scandal can be followed up by the reader elsewhere. Commentators generally agree that Claire did not have a baby by Shelley in Naples: for the rest, opinions differ, and Elise's accusations may have some foundation, as indeed Shelley – half wearily by this time – seems to admit. Certainly he and Claire were together at Este for more than two weeks in 1818, with only Elise and little Allegra for company; and certainly there were great strains throughout these later years between Shelley, Mary and Claire.

Yet the odd fact is that in the history of the English Romantics as a whole, Shelley's second marriage for all its discords and peculiarities remains one of the most enduring and productive. (Compare the domestic failures and frustrations of Coleridge, Hazlitt, or even Byron himself.) In the end his marriage did withstand, or at least accommodate, every strain; and Shelley's understanding of love and its difficulties was immeasurably deepened by the experience. As he joked once to Hunt in 1822: he felt twice as old as his father.

from Julian and Maddalo

The following morn was rainy, cold and dim:
Ere Maddalo arose, I called on him,
And whilst I waited with his child I played;
A lovelier toy sweet Nature never made,
A serious, subtle, wild, yet gentle being,
Graceful without design and unforeseeing,
With eyes – Oh speak not of her eyes! – which seem
Twin mirrors of Italian Heaven, yet gleam
With such deep meaning, as we never see
But in the human countenance: with me
She was a special favourite: I had nursed
Her fine and feeble limbs when she came first
To this bleak world; and she yet seemed to know
On second sight her ancient playfellow,
Less changed than she was by six months or so;
For after her first shyness was worn out
We sate there, rolling billiard balls about,
When the Count entered. Salutations past –
'The word you spoke last night might well have cast
A darkness on my spirit – if man be
The passive thing you say, I should not see
Much harm in the religions and old saws
(Tho' I may never own such leaden laws)
Which break a teachless nature to the yoke:
Mine is another faith' – thus much I spoke
And noting he replied not, added: 'See
This lovely child, blithe, innocent, and free;
She spends a happy time with little care,
While we to such sick thoughts subjected are
As came on you last night – it is our will
That thus enchains us to permitted ill –

[141–171]

We might be otherwise – we might be all
We dream of happy, high, majestical.
Where is the love, beauty, and truth we seek
But in our mind? and if we were not weak
Should we be less in deed than in desire?'
'Ay, if we were not weak – and we aspire
How vainly to be strong!' said Maddalo:
'You talk Utopia.' 'It remains to know,'
I then rejoined, 'and those who try may find
How strong the chains are which our spirit bind;
Brittle perchance as straw . . . We are assured
Much may be conquered, much may be endured,
Of what degrades and crushes us. We know
That we have power over ourselves to do
And suffer – what, we know not till we try;
But something nobler than to live and die –
So taught those kings of old philosophy
Who reigned, before Religion made men blind;
And those who suffer with their suffering kind
Yet feel their faith, religion.' 'My dear friend,'
Said Maddalo, 'my judgement will not bend
To your opinion, though I think you might
Make such a system refutation-tight
As far as words go. I knew one like you
Who to this city came some months ago,
With whom I argued in this sort, and he
Is now gone mad, – and so he answered me –
Poor fellow! but if you would like to go
We'll visit him, and his wild talk will show
How vain are such aspiring theories.'
'I hope to prove the induction otherwise,
And that a want of that true theory, still,
Which seeks a "soul of goodness" in things ill
Or in himself or others, has thus bowed
His being – there are some by nature proud,
Who patient in all else demand but this –
To love and be beloved with gentleness;
And being scorned, what wonder if they die
Some living death? this is not destiny

[172–210]

But man's own wilful ill.'
                    As thus I spoke
Servants announced the gondola, and we
Through the fast-falling rain and high-wrought sea
Sailed to the island where the madhouse stands.
We disembarked. The clap of tortured hands,
Fierce yells and howlings and lamentings keen,
And laughter where complaint had merrier been,
Moans, shrieks, and curses, and blaspheming prayers
Accosted us. We climbed the oozy stairs
Into an old courtyard. I heard on high,
Then, fragments of most touching melody,
But looking up saw not the singer there –
Through the black bars in the tempestuous air
I saw, like weeds on a wrecked palace growing,
Long tangled locks flung wildly forth, and flowing,
Of those who on a sudden were beguiled
Into strange silence, and looked forth and smiled
Hearing sweet sounds. – Then I: 'Methinks there were
A cure of these with patience and kind care,
If music can thus move . . . but what is he
Whom we seek here?' 'Of his sad history
I know but this,' said Maddalo: 'he came
To Venice a dejected man, and fame
Said he was wealthy, or he had been so;
Some thought the loss of fortune wrought him woe;
But he was ever talking in such sort
As you do – far more sadly – he seemed hurt,
Even as a man with his peculiar wrong,
To hear but of the oppression of the strong,
Or those absurd deceits (I think with you
In some respects, you know) which carry through
The excellent impostors of this earth
When they outface detection – he had worth,
Poor fellow! but a humourist in his way' –
'Alas, what drove him mad?' 'I cannot say:
A lady came with him from France, and when
She left him and returned, he wandered then
About yon lonely isles of desert sand

[211–248]

Till he grew wild – he had no cash or land
Remaining, – the police had brought him here –
Some fancy took him and he would not bear
Removal; so I fitted up for him
Those rooms beside the sea, to please his whim,
And sent him busts and books and urns for flowers,
Which had adorned his life in happier hours,
And instruments of music – you may guess
A stranger could do little more or less
For one so gentle and unfortunate:
And those are his sweet strains which charm the weight
From madmen's chains, and make this Hell appear
A heaven of sacred silence, hushed to hear.' –
'Nay, this was kind of you – he had no claim,
As the world says' – 'None – but the very same
Which I on all mankind were I as he
Fallen to such deep reverse; – his melody
Is interrupted – now we hear the din
Of madmen, shriek on shriek, again begin;
Let us now visit him; after this strain
He ever communes with himself again,
And sees nor hears not any.' Having said
These words we called the keeper, and he led
To an apartment opening on the sea –
There the poor wretch was sitting mournfully
Near a piano, his pale fingers twined
One with the other, and the ooze and wind
Rushed through an open casement, and did sway
His hair, and starred it with the brackish spray;
His head was leaning on a music book,
And he was muttering, and his lean limbs shook;
His lips were pressed against a folded leaf
In hue too beautiful for health, and grief
Smiled in their motions as they lay apart –
As one who wrought from his own fervid heart
The eloquence of passion, soon he raised
His sad meek face and eyes lustrous and glazed
And spoke – sometimes as one who wrote, and thought
His words might move some heart that heeded not,

[249–287]

If sent to distant lands: and then as one
Reproaching deeds never to be undone
With wondering self-compassion; then his speech
Was lost in grief, and then his words came each
Unmodulated, cold, expressionless, –
But that from one jarred accent you might guess
It was despair made them so uniform:
And all the while the loud and gusty storm
Hissed through the window, and we stood behind
Stealing his accents from the envious wind
Unseen. I yet remember what he said
Distinctly: such impression his words made.

'Month after month,' he cried, 'to bear this load
And as a jade urged by the whip and goad
To drag life on, which like a heavy chain
Lengthens behind with many a link of pain! –
And not to speak my grief – O, not to dare
To give a human voice to my despair,
But live and move, and, wretched thing! smile on
As if I never went aside to groan,
And wear this mask of falsehood even to those
Who are most dear – not for my own repose –
Alas! no scorn or pain or hate could be
So heavy as that falsehood is to me –
But that I cannot bear more altered faces
Than needs must be, more changed and cold embraces,
More misery, disappointment, and mistrust
To own me for their father . . . Would the dust
Were covered in upon my body now!
That the life ceased to toil within my brow!
And then these thoughts would at the least be fled;
Let us not fear such pain can vex the dead.

'What Power delights to torture us? I know
That to myself I do not wholly owe
What now I suffer, though in part I may.
Alas! none strewed sweet flowers upon the way
Where wandering heedlessly, I met pale Pain

[288–324]

My shadow, which will leave me not again –
If I have erred, there was no joy in error,
But pain and insult and unrest and terror;
I have not as some do, bought penitence
With pleasure, and a dark yet sweet offence,
For then, – if love and tenderness and truth
Had overlived hope's momentary youth,
My creed should have redeemed me from repenting;
But loathèd scorn and outrage unrelenting
Met love excited by far other seeming
Until the end was gained . . . as one from dreaming
Of sweetest peace, I woke, and found my state
Such as it is. –
                     'O Thou, my spirit's mate
Who, for thou art compassionate and wise,
Wouldst pity me from thy most gentle eyes
If this sad writing thou shouldst ever see –
My secret groans must be unheard by thee,
Thou wouldst weep tears bitter as blood to know
Thy lost friend's incommunicable woe.

'Ye few by whom my nature has been weighed
In friendship, let me not that name degrade
By placing on your hearts the secret load
Which crushes mine to dust. There is one road
To peace and that is truth, which follow ye!
Love sometimes leads astray to misery.
Yet think not though subdued – and I may well
Say that I am subdued – that the full Hell
Within me would infect the untainted breast
Of sacred nature with its own unrest;
As some perverted beings think to find
In scorn or hate a medicine for the mind
Which scorn or hate have wounded – O how vain!
The dagger heals not but may rend again . . .
Believe that I am ever still the same
In creed as in resolve, and what may tame
My heart, must leave the understanding free,

Or all would sink in this keen agony –
Nor dream that I will join the vulgar cry;
Or with my silence sanction tyranny;
Or seek a moment's shelter from my pain
In any madness which the world calls gain,
Ambition or revenge or thoughts as stern
As those which make me what I am; or turn
To avarice or misanthropy or lust . . .
Heap on me soon, O grave, thy welcome dust!
Till then the dungeon may demand its prey,
And Poverty and Shame may meet and say –
Halting beside me on the public way –
"That love-devoted youth is ours – let's sit
Beside him – he may live some six months yet."
Or the red scaffold, as our country bends,
May ask some willing victim, or ye friends
May fall under some sorrow which this heart
Or hand may share or vanquish or avert;
I am prepared – in truth with no proud joy –
To do or suffer aught, as when a boy
I did devote to justice and to love
My nature, worthless now! . . .
                            'I must remove
A veil from my pent mind. 'Tis torn aside!
O, pallid as Death's dedicated bride,
Thou mockery which art sitting by my side,
Am I not wan like thee? at the grave's call
I haste, invited to thy wedding-ball
To greet the ghastly paramour, for whom
Thou hast deserted me . . . and made the tomb
Thy bridal bed . . . But I beside your feet
Will lie and watch ye from my winding sheet –
Thus . . . wide awake tho' dead . . . yet stay, O stay!
Go not so soon – I know not what I say –
Hear but my reasons . . . I am mad, I fear,
My fancy is o'erwrought . . . thou art not here . . .
Pale art thou, 'tis most true . . . but thou art gone,
Thy work is finished . . . I am left alone! –

*   *   *

[361–397]

'Nay, was it I who wooed thee to this breast
Which, like a serpent, thou envenomest
As in repayment of the warmth it lent?
Didst thou not seek me for thine own content?
Did not thy love awaken mine? I thought
That thou wert she who said, "You kiss me not
Ever, I fear you do not love me now" –
In truth I loved even to my overthrow
Her, who would fain forget these words; but they
Cling to her mind, and cannot pass away.

* * *

'You say that I am proud – that when I speak
My lip is tortured with the wrongs which break
The spirit it expresses . . . Never one
Humbled himself before, as I have done!
Even the instinctive worm on which we tread
Turns, though it wound not – then with prostrate head
Sinks in the dusk and writhes like me – and dies?
No: wears a living death of agonies!
As the slow shadows of the pointed grass
Mark the eternal periods, his pangs pass
Slow, ever-moving, – making moments be
As mine seem – each an immortality!

* * *

'That you had never seen me – never heard
My voice, and more than all had ne'er endured
The deep pollution of my loathed embrace –
That your eyes ne'er had lied love in my face –
That, like some maniac monk, I had torn out
The nerves of manhood by their bleeding root
With mine own quivering fingers, so that ne'er
Our hearts had for a moment mingled there
To disunite in horror – these were not
With thee, like some suppressed and hideous thought
Which flits athwart our musings, but can find
No rest within a pure and gentle mind . . .
Thou sealedst them with many a bare broad word,
And searedst my memory o'er them, – for I heard
And can forget not . . . they were ministered

One after one, those curses. Mix them up
Like self-destroying poisons in one cup,
And they will make one blessing, which thou ne'er
Didst imprecate for, on me, – death.

                    *   *   *
                                        'It were
A cruel punishment for one most cruel,
If such can love, to make that love the fuel
Of the mind's hell; hate, scorn, remorse, despair:
But *me* – whose heart a stranger's tear might wear
As water-drops the sandy fountain-stone,
Who loved and pitied all things, and could moan
For woes which others hear not, and could see
The absent with the glance of phantasy,
And with the poor and trampled sit and weep,
Following the captive to his dungeon deep;
Me – who am as a nerve o'er which do creep
The else unfelt oppressions of this earth,
And was to thee the flame upon thy hearth,
When all beside was cold – that thou on me
Shouldst rain these plagues of blistering agony –
Such curses are from lips once eloquent
With love's too partial praise – let none relent
Who intend deeds too dreadful for a name
Henceforth, if an example for the same
They seek . . . for thou on me lookedst so, and so –
And didst speak thus . . . and thus . . . I live to show
How much men bear and die not!

               *   *   *
                              'Thou wilt tell,
With the grimace of hate, how horrible
It was to meet my love when thine grew less;
Thou wilt admire how I could e'er address
Such features to love's work . . . this taunt, though true,
(For indeed Nature nor in form nor hue
Bestowed on me her choicest workmanship)
Shall not be thy defence . . . for since thy lip
Met mine first, years long past, since thine eye kindled
With soft fire under mine, I have not dwindled

                                        [435–469]

Nor changed in mind or body, or in aught
But as love changes what it loveth not
After long years and many trials.
                    'How vain
Are words! I thought never to speak again,
Not even in secret, — not to my own heart —
But from my lips the unwilling accents start,
And from my pen the words flow as I write,
Dazzling my eyes with scalding tears . . . my sight
Is dim to see that charactered in vain
On this unfeeling leaf which burns the brain
And eats into it . . . blotting all things fair
And wise and good which time had written there.

'Those who inflict must suffer, for they see
The work of their own hearts, and this must be
Our chastisement or recompense – O child!
I would that thine were like to be more mild
For both our wretched sakes . . . for thine the most
Who feelest already all that thou hast lost
Without the power to wish it thine again;
And as slow years pass, a funereal train
Each with the ghost of some lost hope or friend
Following it like its shadow, wilt thou bend
No thought on my dead memory?
                *   *   *
                        'Alas, love!
Fear me not . . . against thee I would not move
A finger in despite. Do I not live
That thou mayst have less bitter cause to grieve?
I give thee tears for scorn and love for hate;
And that thy lot may be less desolate
Than his on whom thou tramplest, I refrain
From that sweet sleep which medicines all pain.
Then, when thou speakest of me, never say
"He could forgive not." Here I cast away
All human passions, all revenge, all pride;
I think, speak, act no ill; I do but hide
Under these words, like embers, every spark

[470–504]

Of that which has consumed me – quick and dark
The grave is yawning . . . as its roof shall cover
My limbs with dust and worms under and over
So let Oblivion hide this grief . . . the air
Closes upon my accents, as despair
Upon my heart – let death upon despair!'

He ceased, and overcome leant back awhile,
Then rising, with a melancholy smile
Went to a sofa, and lay down, and slept
A heavy sleep, and in his dreams he wept
And muttered some familiar name, and we
Wept without shame in his society.
I think I never was impressed so much;
The man who were not, must have lacked a touch
Of human nature . . . then we lingered not,
Although our argument was quite forgot,
But calling the attendants, went to dine
At Maddalo's; yet neither cheer nor wine
Could give us spirits, for we talked of him
And nothing else, till daylight made stars dim;
And we agreed his was some dreadful ill
Wrought on him boldly, yet unspeakable,
By a dear friend; some deadly change in love
Of one vowed deeply which he dreamed not of;
For whose sake he, it seemed, had fixed a blot
Of falsehood on his mind which flourished not
But in the light of all-beholding truth;
And having stamped this canker on his youth
She had abandoned him – and how much more
Might be his woe, we guessed not – he had store
Of friends and fortune once, as we could guess
From his nice habits and his gentleness;
These were now lost . . . it were a grief indeed
If he had changed one unsustaining reed
For all that such a man might else adorn.
The colours of his mind seemed yet unworn;
For the wild language of his grief was high,
Such as in measure were called poetry;

And I remember one remark which then
Maddalo made. He said: 'Most wretched men
Are cradled into poetry by wrong,
They learn in suffering what they teach in song.'

If I had been an unconnected man
I, from this moment, should have formed some plan
Never to leave sweet Venice, – for to me
It was delight to ride by the lone sea;
And then, the town is silent – one may write
Or read in gondolas by day or night,
Having the little brazen lamp alight,
Unseen, uninterrupted; books are there,
Pictures, and casts from all those statues fair
Which were twin-born with poetry, and all
We seek in towns, with little to recall
Regrets for the green country. I might sit
In Maddalo's great palace, and his wit
And subtle talk would cheer the winter night
And make me know myself, and the firelight
Would flash upon our faces, till the day
Might dawn and make me wonder at my stay:
But I had friends in London too: the chief
Attraction here, was that I sought relief
From the deep tenderness that maniac wrought
Within me – 'twas perhaps an idle thought –
But I imagined that if day by day
I watched him, and but seldom went away,
And studied all the beatings of his heart
With zeal, as men study some stubborn art
For their own good, and could by patience find
An entrance to the caverns of his mind,
I might reclaim him from his dark estate:
In friendships I had been most fortunate –
Yet never saw I one whom I would call
More willingly my friend; and this was all
Accomplished not; such dreams of baseless good
Oft come and go in crowds or solitude
And leave no trace – but what I now designed

[543–580]

Made for long years impression on my mind.
The following morning, urged by my affairs,
I left bright Venice . . .

The Hoppner scandal

Ravenna: August 7. 1821. –

My dearest Mary

I arrived last night at 10 oClock & sate up last night talking with Lord Byron until 5 this morning. – I then went to sleep, & now awake at eleven, and having dispatched my breakfast as quick as possible, mean to devote the interval until 12 when the post departs to you. –

Lord Byron is very well, & was delighted to see me. He has in fact completely recovered his health, & lives a life totally the reverse of that which he led at Venice. He has a permanent sort of liaison with Contessa Guiccioli, who is now at Florence, & seems from her letters to be a very aimiable woman. She is waiting there until something shall be decided as to their emigration to Switzerland or stay in Italy: which is yet undetermined on either side. – She was compelled to escape from the Papal territory in great haste, as measures had already been taken to place her in a Convent where she would have been unrelentingly confined for life. The oppression of the marriage compact, as existing in the laws & opinions of Italy, though less frequently exercised is far severer than that of England. – I tremble to think of what poor Emilia is destined to. – Lord Byron had almost destroyed himself at Venice: his state of debility was such that he was unable to digest any food – he was consumed by hectic fever, and would speedily have perished but for this attachment which reclaimed him from the excesses into which he threw himself from carelessness & pride rather than taste. – Poor fellow – he is now quite well and immersed in politics & literature. He has given me a number of the most interesting details on the former subject – but we will not speak of them in a letter. – Fletcher is here, & as if like a shadow he waxed & waned with the substance of his master, Fletcher also has recovered his good lookes & from amidst the unseasonable grey hairs a fresh harvest of flaxen locks put forth. –

We talked a great deal of poetry & such matters last night: & as usual differed & I think more than ever. – He affects to patronize a system of criticism fit only for the production of mediocrity, & although all his fine poems & passages have been produced in defiance of this system: yet I recognize the pernicious effects of it in the 'Doge of Venice', & it will cramp & limit his future efforts however great they may be unless he gets rid of it. I have read only parts of it, or rather he himself read them to me & gave me the plan of the whole. – Allegra, he says, is grown very beautiful: but he complains that her temper is violent and imperious. – He has no intention of leaving her in Italy; indeed the thing is too improper in itself not to carry condemnation along with it. Contessa Guiccioli he says is very fond of her: indeed I cannot see why *she* should not take care of it, if she is to live as his ostensible mistress. – all this I shall know more of soon.

Lord Byron has also told me a circumstance that shocks me exceedingly, because it exhibits a degree of desperate & wicked malice for which I am at a loss to account. When I hear such things my patience & my philosophy are put to a severe proof, whilst I refrain from seeking out some obscure hiding place where the countenance of man may never meet me more. It seems that *Elise*, actuated either by some inconceivable malice for our dismissing her – or bribed by my enemies – or making common cause with her infamous husband has persuaded the Hoppners of a story so monstrous & incredible that they must have been prone to believe any evil to have believed such assertions upon such evidence. Mr Hoppner wrote to Lord B[yron] to state this story as the reason why *he* declined any further communication with me, & why he advised him to do the same. Elise says that Clare was my mistress – that is all very well & so far there is nothing new: all the world has heard so much & people may believe or not believe as they think good. – She then proceeds to say that Clare was with child by me – that I gave her the most violent medicines to procure abortion – that [I did not *cancelled*] this not succeeding she was brought to bed & that I immediately tore the child from her & sent it to the foundling hospital – I quote Mr Hoppners words – and this is stated to have happened in the winter after we left Este. In addition she says that both I & Clare treated *you* in the most shameful manner – that I neglected & beat you, & that Clare never let a day pass without offering you insults of the most violent kind in which she was abetted by me. – As to what Reviews & the world says I do not care a jot; but when persons who have known me are capable of conceiving of me – not that I have fallen into a great error & imprudence as would have been the living with Clare as my mistress – but that I have committed such unutterable crimes as destroying or abandoning a child – & that my own – imagine my despair of good – imagine how it is possible that one of so weak & sensitive a nature as mine can run further the gauntlet through this hellish society of men. – [*Three lines are here heavily cancelled*] You should write to the Hoppners a letter refuting the charge in case you believe & know & can prove that it is false: stating the grounds & the proofs of your belief. – I need not dictate what you should say, nor I hope inspire you with warmth to rebut a charge which you only can effectually rebut. – If you will send the letter to me here, I will forward it to the Hoppners. – Lord Byron is not up, I do not know the Hoppners address – & I am anxious not to lose the post.

[*A line is heavily scored through, and the MS. ends here*]

6

Eternal Image

Introduction

WITH THE IMMINENT APPROACH of Shelley's death in 1822, it is natural to cast around through his writing for work which might sum up his whole attitude to life and love. In a sense this is a mistaken search, for his biography reveals no feeling of achieved position, of calm retrospective, but only continuous complication and activity, right to the very end. In the month of his death one can see, for example, at least four areas in which he was pressing forward into the unknown. He had the first part of a major philosophic poem in draft, *The Triumph of Life*, which promised to outstrip even *Prometheus Unbound*. He had the publishing scheme for *The Liberal*, which Leigh Hunt had just come over to edit with Byron at Livorno (four issues were eventually produced, with essays from Hazlitt, poetry from Byron, verse translation from Shelley, and ghost stories by Mary.) He was deeply involved in a Platonic affair with Jane Williams, for whom he was writing a number of remarkable lyric poems. His relations with Mary and Claire were obviously about to reach one of their periodic flashpoints – a crisis which could not have endured the hypnotic intimacy of their seaside life at Casa Magni much beyond September, whatever had happened. There was still in fact very little that was stable or unquestioned in his life, and no sense in his work that he had solved any of the great mysteries of love.

Yet he had expressed them. This final section gives a number of passages, mainly from the last eighteen months of his life, in which Shelley does seem for a moment to stand back from his experience and attempt some sort of summation, to reach for a philosophic or symbolic truth, to find an eternal image. Though it is perhaps relevant to recall that haunting warning from *Prometheus Unbound*:

> . . . But a voice
> Is wanting, the deep truth is imageless;
> For what would it avail to bid thee gaze
> On the revolving world? What to bid speak
> Fate, Time, Occasion, Chance and Change? To these
> All things are subject but eternal Love.
>
> [Act II, Scene 4, ll. 115–20]

The first extract comes from his *Defence of Poetry*, written at Pisa in February and March 1821. It is still not generally known that this essay is already something of an anthology culled from his previous writings, drawing on the Prefaces to his previous volumes of poetry, his essays on Christianity, the *Symposium*, and the Devil, and most notably on his fine political pamphlet *A Philosophical View of Reform* (1820). The famous peroration to the *Defence*, that poets 'are the unacknowledged legislators of the world', actually originated in this essay, and the entire closing paragraph is taken from it. More clearly than anywhere else however, Shelley places the notion of love at the centre of his conception of the moral imagination: 'The great secret of morals is love, or a going out of our own nature and an identification of ourselves with the beautiful which exists in thought, action, or person, not our own.' He also identifies the 'Christian and chivalric systems' of love with the main European development of poetry, which produced Dante, Petrarch, Shakespeare, and 'the great writers of our own age'. It is interesting to find Shelley here finally speaking of religion in a cultural rather than a theological way, and finding his own notion of 'the true relation borne to each other by the sexes' firmly within such a tradition.

The three Prefaces to *Epipsychidion* are given in full, since although they were written at about the same time at Pisa, they already seem to foresee the last retreat to the solitary bay of Lerici (the Casa Magni appears in the disguise of a Saracen castle) and even the drowning, 'as he was preparing a voyage to one of the wildest of the Sporades'. This is the last vision of Shelley's ideal community of lovers, which is given its most visionary expression towards the end of the poem. The *Epipsychidion* is perhaps the nearest thing we have to a *summa* of his views on love. In a way this entire anthology is merely a preparation for an understanding of the diverse elements that went into this most Shelleyan of poems: fiery, rebellious, dreamy, despairing, visionary, polemical, sensuous, sublime, philosophical, and swift, all at the same time; and with certain unmistakable touches of self-mocking humour too:

> Then, from the caverns of my dreamy youth
> I sprang, as one sandalled with plumes of fire,
> And towards the lodestar of my one desire,
> I flitted, like a dizzy moth, whose flight
> Is as a dead leaf's in the owlet light, . . .

At one level, *Epipsychidion* is quite simply and openly an autobiography of Shelley's love-life from the time he was at Oxford until the time he met Emilia Viviani, a beautiful nineteen-year-old heiress whom Mary and Claire had befriended at Pisa in the spring of 1821. In this sense it is a *poème à clef*, describing the various stages of growth in his philosophy, and the various women with whom he fell in love along the way; the whole poem being presented in terms of a journey. The main figures are exactly those one would expect from his biography, and each is identified by a cosmological symbol, in the tradition of Petrarchan courtly love. Mary Shelley is the Moon; Harriet Shelley is 'the Planet of that Hour'; Emilia is the Sun; and Claire Clairmont is the Comet, 'beautiful and fierce'.

Other identities are more deliberately ambiguous. The three ladies early on in his life who were respectively 'fair', 'wise' and 'true', have been variously identified with Harriet Grove, Elizabeth Hitchener, Cornelia Boinville, Harriet Shelley again, and even Fanny Godwin (who had also committed suicide in 1816). The evil woman who 'Sate by a well, under blue nightshade bowers', is generally thought to have been a prostitute whom Shelley met at Oxford, or immediately after his expulsion, when he lived in lodgings in Poland Street, Soho. It is notable that she is associated with a singing voice 'of venomed melody'. The 'Tempest' who blotted out the Moon during the 1816–17 period has never been convincingly named: Eliza Westbrook, Harriet's vengeful sister, has been suggested, but Shelley was never on terms of amorous intimacy with her. Unless it was someone among Shelley's shifting household of servants at Marlow, or some visitor from the Hunt circle – but there is absolutely no indication of this – then biographically the only possible identification is again Claire. It is perhaps suggestive that Shelley's life-long interest in scientific phenomena would have led him to believe the contemporary meteorological theories that *comets* brought disturbances of the upper air, earthquakes and eruptions on land, and storms at sea. The one figure who we look for in vain is Shelley's mother: there seems no recognition whatever of a maternal influence, and this sad absence takes us back to the opening section of the anthology. A psychologist might perhaps suggest that the ariel

> . . . Being whom my spirit oft
> Met on its visioned wanderings, far aloft,
> In the clear golden prime of my youth's dawn, . . .

owed something of her origins to a boyhood starved of more substantial and earthly affections.

In the poet of *Epipsychidion*, who recollects emotions in rapturous anticipation rather than tranquillity, we can also recognize the enthusiast of the free love Note, as well as the driven poet of *Alastor*, the tortured Madman of *Julian and Maddalo* and the Platonist of Bagni di Lucca. The passage opening 'I was never attached to that great sect . . .' restates, once and for all, his hostility to a narrow monogamous attitude to love – 'though it is in the code/ Of modern morals' – and delivers his last, most celebrated animadversion on matrimony, sharpened to a single mocking, classical couplet:

> With one chained friend, perhaps a jealous foe,
> The dreariest and the longest journey go.

Shelley never did of course take Emilia Viviani off to that wonderfully enchanted island, with its East-facing chambers, its books and music, and pebble-paven shore: instead he took Mary, Claire and the Williamses to the beach-house at Lerici. But how long this had been in his mind – as 'a pure anticipated cognition' – is shown by the next extract, a letter to Mary of August 1821 in which the idea has already taken practical shape. Shelley tried both the alternative forms of existence suggested in this letter during his last months. But neither seems to have curbed or satisfied his restless spirit.

The reader will want to look at the many love poems he wrote to Jane Williams during his last weeks, and the long visionary letters he wrote home to his friends in London, John Gisborne especially. But for the purposes of this anthology, two brief, penultimate extracts from those letters to Gisborne on the subject of the *Epipsychidion* come the nearest to a valediction to love.

Finally, as an *envoi*, I have included his Note on a sculpture of Venus Anadyomene, the Goddess of Love rising from the waters, since it takes us back to the opening section of this book, and reminds us how Shelley's love was consummated, with haunting poetic force and sadness, in the wild embrace of the summer sea.

Poetry and love

. . . Poetry lifts the veil from the hidden beauty of the world and makes familiar objects be as if they were not familiar; it reproduces all that it represents, and the impersonations clothed in its Elysian light stand thenceforward in the minds of those who have once contemplated them as memorials of that gentle and exalted content which extends itself over all thoughts and actions with which it coexists. The great secret of morals is love, or a going out of our own nature and an identification of ourselves with the beautiful which exists in thought, action, or person, not our own. A man, to be greatly good, must imagine intensely and comprehensively; he must put himself in the place of another and of many others; the pains and pleasures of his species must become his own. The great instrument of moral good is the imagination: and poetry administers to the effect by acting upon the cause. Poetry enlarges the circumference of the imagination by replenishing it with thoughts of ever new delight, which have the power of attracting and assimilating to their own nature all other thoughts and which form new intervals and interstices whose void forever craves fresh food. Poetry strengthens that faculty which is the organ of the moral nature of man in the same manner as exercise strengthens a limb . . .

*   *   *

It was not until the eleventh century that the effects of the poetry of the Christian and chivalric systems began to manifest themselves. The principle of equality had been discovered and applied by Plato in his *Republic* as the theoretical rule of the mode in which the materials of pleasure and of power produced by the common skill and labour of human beings ought to be distributed among them. The limitations of this rule were asserted by him to be determined only by the sensibility of each, or the utility to result to all. Plato, following the doctrines of Timaeus and Pythagoras, taught also a moral and intellectual system of doctrine, comprehending at once the past, the present, and the future condition of man. Jesus Christ divulged the sacred and eternal truths contained in these views to mankind, and Christianity in its abstract purity became the exoteric expression of the esoteric doctrines of the poetry and wisdom of antiquity. The incorporation of the Celtic nations with the exhausted population of the south impressed upon it the figure of the poetry existing in their mythology and institutions. The result was a sum of the action and reaction of all the causes included in it; for it may be assumed as a maxim that no nation or religion can supersede any other without incorporating into itself a portion of that which it supersedes. The abolition of personal and domestic slavery and the emancipation of women from a great part of the degrading restraints of antiquity were among the consequences of these events.

The abolition of personal slavery is the basis of the highest political hope that it can enter into the mind of man to conceive. The freedom of women produced the poetry of sexual love. Love became a religion the idols of whose worship were ever present. It was as if the statues of Apollo and the Muses had been endowed with life and motion and had walked forth among their worshippers; so that earth became peopled by the inhabitants of a diviner world. The familiar appearance and proceedings of life became wonderful and heavenly, and a paradise was created as out of the wrecks of Eden. And as this creation itself is poetry, so its creators were poets; and language was the instrument of their art: 'Galeotto fù il libro, e chi lo scrisse.'* The Provençal Trouveurs, or inventors, preceded Petrarch, whose verses are as spells which unseal the inmost enchanted fountains of the delight which is in the grief of love. It is impossible to feel them without becoming a portion of that beauty which we contemplate; it were

---

* 'Galeotto was the book, and he who wrote it.' – Dante, *Inferno* [*ed.*]

superfluous to explain how the gentleness and the elevation of mind connected with these sacred emotions can render men more amiable, and generous, and wise, and lift them out of the dull vapours of the little world of self. Dante understood the secret things of love even more than Petrarch. His *Vita Nuova* is an inexhaustible fountain of purity of sentiment and language; it is the idealized history of that period and those intervals of his life which were dedicated to love. His apotheosis of Beatrice in Paradise, and the gradations of his own love and her loveliness, by which as by steps he feigns himself to have ascended to the throne of the Supreme Cause, is the most glorious imagination of modern poetry. The acutest critics have justly reversed the judgement of the vulgar and the order of the great acts of the *Divina Commedia* in the measure of the admiration which they accord to the Hell, Purgatory, and Paradise. The latter is a perpetual hymn of everlasting love. Love, which found a worthy poet in Plato alone of all the ancients, has been celebrated by a chorus of the greatest writers of the renovated world; and the music has penetrated the caverns of society and its echoes still drown the dissonance of arms and superstition. At successive intervals Ariosto, Tasso, Shakespeare, Spenser, Calderon, Rousseau, and the great writers of our own age have celebrated the dominion of love, planting as it were trophies in the human mind of that sublimest victory over sensuality and force. The true relation borne to each other by the sexes into which human kind is distributed has become less misunderstood; and if the error which confounded diversity with inequality of the powers of the two sexes has been partially recognized in the opinions and institutions of modern Europe, we owe this great benefit to the worship of which chivalry was the law, and poets the prophets.

Epipsychidion: *four versions of an explanation*

PREFACE I

The following Poem was found amongst other papers in the Portfolio of a young Englishman with whom the Editor had contracted an intimacy at Florence, brief indeed, but sufficiently long to render the Catastrophe by which it terminated one of the most painful events of his life. –

The literary merit of the Poem in question may not be considerable; but worse verses are printed every day, & He was an accomplished & amiable person but his error was, θνητος ὤν μη θνητα φρονειν,* – his fate is an additional proof that 'The tree of Knowledge is not that of Life.' – He had framed to himself certain opinions, founded no doubt upon the truth of things, but built up to a Babel height; they fell by their own weight, & the thoughts that were his architects, became unintelligible one to the other, as men upon whom confusion of tongues has fallen.

[These] verses seem to have been written as a sort of dedication of some work to have been presented to the person whom they address: but his papers afford no trace of such a work – The circumstances to which [they] the poem allude, may easily be understood by those to whom [the] spirit of the poem itself is [un]intelligible: a detail of facts, sufficiently romantic in [themselves but] their combinations

The melancholy [task] charge of consigning the body of my poor friend to the grave, was committed to me by his

---

* 'Being mortal, not to think like a mortal' (cf. Euripides, *Alcestis* 799 and *Bacchae* 395–6). This implies rivalling the Gods, a dangerous and usually fatal mistake. [*ed.*]

desolated family. I caused him to be buried in a spot selected by himself, & on the h [   ]

PREFACE II

[Epips] T. E. V. Epipsych
Lines addressed to
the Noble Lady
[Emilia] [E. V.]
Emilia

[The following Poem was found in the PF. of a young Englishman, who died on his passage from Leghorn to the Levant. He had bought one of the Sporades] He was accompanied by a lady [who might have been] supposed to be his wife, & an effeminate looking youth, to whom he shewed an [attachment] so [singular] excessive an attachment as to give rise to the suspicion, that she was a woman – At his death this suspicion was confirmed; [   ] object speedily found a refuge both from the taunts of the brute multitude, and from the [   ] of her grief in the same grave that contained her lover. – He had bought one of the Sporades, & fitted up a Saracenic castle which accident had preserved in some repair with simple elegance, & it was his intention to dedicate the remainder of his life to undisturbed intercourse with his companions

These verses apparently were intended as a dedication of a longer poem or series of poems

PREFACE III

The writer of these lines died at Florence in [January 1820] while he was preparing for one of the wildest of the Sporades, where he bought & fitted up the ruins of some old building – His life was singular, less on account of the romantic vicissitudes which diversified it, than the ideal tinge which they received from his own character & feelings –

The verses were apparently intended by the writer to accompany some longer poem or collection of poems, of which there [are no remnants in his] remains [in his] portfolio. –

The editor is induced to [   ]

The present poem, like the vita Nova of Dante, is sufficiently intelligible to a certain class of readers without a matter of fact history of the circumstances to which it relate, & to a certain other class, it must & ought ever to remain incomprehensible – It was evidently intended to be prefixed to a longer poem or series of poems – but among his papers there are no traces of such a collection.

ADVERTISEMENT

The Writer of the following lines died at Florence, as he was preparing for a voyage to one of the wildest of the Sporades, which he had bought, and where he had fitted up the ruins of an old building, and where it was his hope to have realized a scheme of life, suited perhaps to that happier and better world of which he is now an inhabitant, but hardly practicable in this. His life was singular; less on account of the romantic vicissitudes which diversified it, than the ideal tinge which it received from his own character and feelings. The present Poem, like the *Vita Nuova* of Dante, is sufficiently intelligible to a certain class of readers without a matter-of-fact history of the circumstances to which it relates; and to a certain other class it must ever remain incomprehensible, from a defect of a common organ of perception for the ideas of which it treats. Not but that *gran vergogna sarebbe a colui, che rimasse cosa sotto veste di figura, o di colore rettorico: e domandato non sapesse denudare le sue parole da cotal veste, in guisa che avessero verace intendimento.**

---

* 'It would be a great shame for a man to rhyme under cover of a figure or rhetorical colour; and then afterwards, when asked, not to know how to strip his words of that clothing, in such a way that they should have a true meaning.' – *Vita Nuova* [ed.]

The present poem appears to have been intended by the Writer as the dedication to some longer one. The stanza on the opposite page* is almost a literal translation from Dante's famous Canzone

Voi, ch' intendendo, il terzo ciel movete, etc.

The presumptuous application of the concluding lines to his own composition will raise a smile at the expense of my unfortunate friend: be it a smile not of contempt, but pity.

S.

> My Song, I fear that thou wilt find but few
> Who fitly shall conceive thy reasoning,
> Of such hard matter dost thou entertain;
> Whence, if by misadventure, chance should bring
> Thee to base company (as chance may do),
> Quite unaware of what thou dost contain,
> I prithee, comfort thy sweet self again,
> My last delight! tell them that they are dull,
> And bid them own that thou art beautiful.

---

* of the original edition, here printed immediately following. [*ed.*]

from Epipsychidion

She met me, Stranger, upon life's rough way,
And lured me towards sweet Death; as Night by Day,
Winter by Spring, or Sorrow by swift Hope,
Led into light, life, peace. An antelope,
In the suspended impulse of its lightness,
Were less aethereally light: the brightness
Of her divinest presence trembles through
Her limbs, as underneath a cloud of dew
Embodied in the windless heaven of June
Amid the splendour-wingèd stars, the Moon
Burns, inextinguishably beautiful:
And from her lips, as from a hyacinth full
Of honey-dew, a liquid murmur drops,
Killing the sense with passion; sweet as stops
Of planetary music heard in trance.
In her mild lights the starry spirits dance,
The sunbeams of those wells which ever leap
Under the lightnings of the soul – too deep
For the brief fathom-line of thought or sense.
The glory of her being, issuing thence,
Stains the dead, blank, cold air with a warm shade
Of unentangled intermixture, made
By Love, of light and motion: one intense
Diffusion, one serene Omnipresence,
Whose flowing outlines mingle in their flowing,
Around her cheeks and utmost fingers glowing
With the unintermitted blood, which there
Quivers, (as in a fleece of snow-like air
The crimson pulse of living morning quiver,)
Continuously prolonged, and ending never,
Till they are lost, and in that Beauty furled

Which penetrates and clasps and fills the world;
Scarce visible from extreme loveliness.
Warm fragrance seems to fall from her light dress
And her loose hair; and where some heavy tress
The air of her own speed has disentwined,
The sweetness seems to satiate the faint wind;
And in the soul a wild odour is felt,
Beyond the sense, like fiery dews that melt
Into the bosom of a frozen bud. –
See where she stands! a mortal shape indued
With love and life and light and deity,
And motion which may change but cannot die;
An image of some bright Eternity;
A shadow of some golden dream; a Splendour
Leaving the third sphere pilotless; a tender
Reflection of the eternal Moon of Love
Under whose motions life's dull billows move;
A Metaphor of Spring and Youth and Morning;
A Vision like incarnate April, warning,
With smiles and tears, Frost the Anatomy
Into his summer grave.
                              Ah, woe is me!
What have I dared? where am I lifted? how
Shall I descend, and perish not? I know
That Love makes all things equal: I have heard
By mine own heart this joyous truth averred:
The spirit of the worm beneath the sod
In love and worship, blends itself with God.

Spouse! Sister! Angel! Pilot of the Fate
Whose course has been so starless! O too late
Belovèd! O too soon adored, by me!
For in the fields of Immortality
My spirit should at first have worshipped thine,
A divine presence in a place divine;
Or should have moved beside it on this earth,
A shadow of that substance, from its birth;
But not as now: – I love thee; yes, I feel
That on the fountain of my heart a seal

Is set, to keep its waters pure and bright
For thee, since in those *tears* thou hast delight.
We – are we not formed, as notes of music are,
For one another, though dissimilar;
Such difference without discord, as can make
Those sweetest sounds, in which all spirits shake
As trembling leaves in a continuous air?

Thy wisdom speaks in me, and bids me dare
Beacon the rocks on which high hearts are wrecked.
I never was attached to that great sect,
Whose doctrine is, that each one should select
Out of the crowd a mistress or a friend,
And all the rest, though fair and wise, commend
To cold oblivion, though it is in the code
Of modern morals, and the beaten road
Which those poor slaves with weary footsteps tread,
Who travel to their home among the dead
By the broad highway of the world, and so
With one chained friend, perhaps a jealous foe,
The dreariest and the longest journey go.

True Love in this differs from gold and clay,
That to divide is not to take away.
Love is like understanding, that grows bright,
Gazing on many truths; 'tis like thy light,
Imagination! which from earth and sky,
And from the depths of human fantasy,
As from a thousand prisms and mirrors, fills
The Universe with glorious beams, and kills
Error, the worm, with many a sun-like arrow
Of its reverberated lightning. Narrow
The heart that loves, the brain that contemplates,
The life that wears, the spirit that creates
One object, and one form, and builds thereby
A sepulchre for its eternity.

Mind from its object differs most in this:
Evil from good; misery from happiness;

[140–175]

The baser from the nobler; the impure
And frail, from what is clear and must endure.
If you divide suffering and dross, you may
Diminish till it is consumed away;
If you divide pleasure and love and thought,
Each part exceeds the whole; and we know not
How much, while any yet remains unshared,
Of pleasure may be gained, of sorrow spared:
This truth is that deep well, whence sages draw
The unenvied light of hope; the eternal law
By which those live, to whom this world of life
Is as a garden ravaged, and whose strife
Tills for the promise of a later birth
The wilderness of this Elysian earth.

There was a Being whom my spirit oft
Met on its visioned wanderings, far aloft,
In the clear golden prime of my youth's dawn,
Upon the fairy isles of sunny lawn,
Amid the enchanted mountains, and the caves
Of divine sleep, and on the air-like waves
Of wonder-level dream, whose tremulous floor
Paved her light steps; – on an imagined shore,
Under the gray beak of some promontory
She met me, robed in such exceeding glory,
That I beheld her not. In solitudes
Her voice came to me through the whispering woods,
And from the fountains, and the odours deep
Of flowers, which, like lips murmuring in their sleep
Of the sweet kisses which had lulled them there,
Breathed but of *her* to the enamoured air;
And from the breezes whether low or loud,
And from the rain of every passing cloud,
And from the singing of the summer-birds,
And from all sounds, all silence. In the words
Of antique verse and high romance, – in form,
Sound, colour – in whatever checks that Storm
Which with the shattered present chokes the past;
And in that best philosophy, whose taste

[176–213]

Makes this cold common hell, our life, a doom
As glorious as a fiery martyrdom;
Her Spirit was the harmony of truth. –

    Then, from the caverns of my dreamy youth
I sprang, as one sandalled with plumes of fire,
And towards the lodestar of my one desire,
I flitted, like a dizzy moth, whose flight
Is as a dead leaf's in the owlet light,
When it would seek in Hesper's setting sphere
A radiant death, a fiery sepulchre,
As if it were a lamp of earthly flame. –
But She, whom prayers or tears then could not tame,
Passed, like a God throned on a wingèd planet,
Whose burning plumes to tenfold swiftness fan it,
Into the dreary cone of our life's shade;
And as a man with mighty loss dismayed,
I would have followed, though the grave between
Yawned like a gulf whose spectres are unseen:
When a voice said: – 'O thou of hearts the weakest,
The phantom is beside thee whom thou seekest.'
Then I – 'Where!' – the world's echo answered 'where?'
And in that silence, and in my despair,
I questioned every tongueless wind that flew
Over my tower of mourning, if it knew
Whither 'twas fled, this soul out of my soul;
And murmured names and spells which have control
Over the sightless tyrants of our fate;
But neither prayer nor verse could dissipate
The night which closed on her; nor uncreate
That world within this Chaos, mine and me,
Of which she was the veiled Divinity,
The world I say of thoughts that worshipped her:
And therefore I went forth, with hope and fear
And every gentle passion sick to death,
Feeding my course with expectation's breath,
Into the wintry forest of our life;
And struggling through its error with vain strife,
And stumbling in my weakness and my haste,

And half bewildered by new forms, I passed,
Seeking among those untaught foresters
If I could find one form resembling hers,
In which she might have masked herself from me.
There, – One, whose voice was venomed melody
Sate by a well, under blue nightshade bowers;
The breath of her false mouth was like faint flowers,
Her touch was as electric poison, – flame
Out of her looks into my vitals came,
And from her living cheeks and bosom flew
A killing air, which pierced like honey-dew
Into the core of my green heart, and lay
Upon its leaves; until, as hair grown gray
O'er a young brow, they hid its unblown prime
With ruins of unseasonable time.

In many mortal forms I rashly sought
The shadow of that idol of my thought.
And some were fair – but beauty dies away:
Others were wise – but honeyed words betray:
And One was true – oh! why not true to me?
Then, as a hunted deer that could not flee,
I turned upon my thoughts, and stood at bay,
Wounded and weak and panting; the cold day
Trembled, for pity of my strife and pain.
When, like a noonday dawn, there shone again
Deliverance. One stood on my path who seemed
As like the glorious shape which I had dreamed
As is the Moon, whose changes ever run
Into themselves, to the eternal Sun;
The cold chaste Moon, the Queen of Heaven's bright isles,
Who makes all beautiful on which she smiles,
That wandering shrine of soft yet icy flame
Which ever is transformed, yet still the same,
And warms not but illumines. Young and fair
As the descended Spirit of that sphere,
She hid me, as the Moon may hide the night
From its own darkness, until all was bright
Between the Heaven and Earth of my calm mind,

[252–289]

And, as a cloud charioted by the wind,
She led me to a cave in that wild place,
And sate beside me, with her downward face
Illumining my slumbers, like the Moon
Waxing and waning o'er Endymion.
And I was laid asleep, spirit and limb,
And all my being became bright or dim
As the Moon's image in a summer sea,
According as she smiled or frowned on me;
And there I lay, within a chaste cold bed:
Alas, I then was nor alive nor dead; –
For at her silver voice came Death and Life,
Unmindful each of their accustomed strife,
Masked like twin babes, a sister and a brother,
The wandering hopes of one abandoned mother,
And through the cavern without wings they flew,
And cried 'Away, he is not of our crew.'
I wept, and though it be a dream, I weep.

What storms then shook the ocean of my sleep,
Blotting that Moon, whose pale and waning lips
Then shrank as in the sickness of eclipse; –
And how my soul was as a lampless sea,
And who was then its Tempest; and when She,
The Planet of that hour, was quenched, what frost
Crept o'er those waters, till from coast to coast
The moving billows of my being fell
Into a death of ice, immovable; –
And then – what earthquakes made it gape and split,
The white Moon smiling all the while on it,
These words conceal: – If not, each word would be
The key of staunchless tears. Weep not for me!

At length, into the obscure Forest came
The Vision I had sought through grief and shame.
Athwart that wintry wilderness of thorns
Flashed from her motion splendour like the Morn's,
And from her presence life was radiated
Through the gray earth and branches bare and dead;

So that her way was paved, and roofed above
With flowers as soft as thoughts of budding love;
And music from her respiration spread
Like light, – all other sounds were penetrated
By the small, still, sweet spirit of that sound,
So that the savage winds hung mute around;
And odours warm and fresh fell from her hair
Dissolving the dull cold in the frore air:
Soft as an Incarnation of the Sun,
When light is changed to love, this glorious One
Floated into the cavern where I lay,
And called my Spirit, and the dreaming clay
Was lifted by the thing that dreamed below
As smoke by fire, and in her beauty's glow
I stood, and felt the dawn of my long night
Was penetrating me with living light:
I knew it was the Vision veiled from me
So many years – that it was Emily.

Twin Spheres of light who rule this passive Earth,
This world of love, this *me*; and into birth
Awaken all its fruits and flowers, and dart
Magnetic might into its central heart;
And lift its billows and its mists, and guide
By everlasting laws, each wind and tide
To its fit cloud, and its appointed cave;
And lull its storms, each in the craggy grave
Which was its cradle, luring to faint bowers
The armies of the rainbow-wingèd showers;
And, as those married lights, which from the towers
Of Heaven look forth and fold the wandering globe
In liquid sleep and splendour, as a robe;
And all their many-mingled influence blend,
If equal, yet unlike, to one sweet end: –
So ye, bright regents, with alternate sway
Govern my sphere of being, night and day!
Thou, not disdaining even a borrowed might;
Thou, not eclipsing a remoter light;
And, through the shadow of the seasons three,

From Spring to Autumn's sere maturity,
Light it into the Winter of the tomb,
Where it may ripen to a brighter bloom.
Thou too, O Comet beautiful and fierce,
Who drew the heart of this frail Universe
Towards thine own; till, wrecked in that convulsion,
Alternating attraction and repulsion,
Thine went astray and that was rent in twain;
Oh, float into our azure heaven again!
Be there Love's folding-star at thy return;
The living Sun will feed thee from its urn
Of golden fire; the Moon will veil her horn
In thy last smiles; adoring Even and Morn
Will worship thee with incense of calm breath
And lights and shadows; as the star of Death
And Birth is worshipped by those sisters wild
Called Hope and Fear – upon the heart are piled
Their offerings, – of this sacrifice divine
A World shall be the altar.
                                        Lady mine,
Scorn not these flowers of thought, the fading birth
Which from its heart of hearts that plant puts forth
Whose fruit, made perfect by thy sunny eyes,
Will be as of the trees of Paradise.

    The day is come, and thou wilt fly with me.
To whatsoe'er of dull mortality
Is mine, remain a vestal sister still;
To the intense, the deep, the imperishable,
Not mine but me, henceforth be thou united
Even as a bride, delighting and delighted.
The hour is come: – the destined Star has risen
Which shall descend upon a vacant prison.
The walls are high, the gates are strong, thick set
The sentinels – but true Love never yet
Was thus constrained: it overleaps all fence:
Like lightning, with invisible violence
Piercing its continents; like Heaven's free breath,
Which he who grasps can hold not; liker Death,

Who rides upon a thought, and makes his way
Through temple, tower, and palace, and the array
Of arms: more strength has Love than he or they;
For it can burst his charnel, and make free
The limbs in chains, the heart in agony,
The soul in dust and chaos.
                     Emily,
A ship is floating in the harbour now,
A wind is hovering o'er the mountain's brow;
There is a path on the sea's azure floor,
No keel has ever ploughed that path before;
The halcyons brood around the foamless isles;
The treacherous Ocean has forsworn its wiles;
The merry mariners are bold and free:
Say, my heart's sister, wilt thou sail with me?
Our bark is as an albatross, whose nest
Is a far Eden of the purple East;
And we between her wings will sit, while Night,
And Day, and Storm, and Calm, pursue their flight,
Our ministers, along the boundless Sea,
Treading each other's heels, unheededly.
It is an isle under Ionian skies,
Beautiful as a wreck of Paradise,
And, for the harbours are not safe and good,
This land would have remained a solitude
But for some pastoral people native there,
Who from the Elysian, clear, and golden air
Draw the last spirit of the age of gold,
Simple and spirited; innocent and bold.
The blue Aegean girds this chosen home,
With ever-changing sound and light and foam,
Kissing the sifted sands, and caverns hoar;
And all the winds wandering along the shore
Undulate with the undulating tide:
There are thick woods where sylvan forms abide;
And many a fountain, rivulet, and pond,
As clear as elemental diamond,
Or serene morning air; and far beyond,
The mossy tracks made by the goats and deer

[402–439]

(Which the rough shepherd treads but once a year)
Pierce into glades, caverns, and bowers, and halls
Built round with ivy, which the waterfalls
Illumining, with sound that never fails
Accompany the noonday nightingales;
And all the place is peopled with sweet airs;
The light clear element which the isle wears
Is heavy with the scent of lemon-flowers,
Which floats like mist laden with unseen showers,
And falls upon the eyelids like faint sleep;
And from the moss violets and jonquils peep,
And dart their arrowy odour through the brain
Till you might faint with that delicious pain.
And every motion, odour, beam, and tone,
With that deep music is in unison:
Which is a soul within the soul – they seem
Like echoes of an antenatal dream. –
It is an isle 'twixt Heaven, Air, Earth, and Sea,
Cradled, and hung in clear tranquillity;
Bright as that wandering Eden Lucifer,
Washed by the soft blue Oceans of young air.
It is a favoured place. Famine or Blight,
Pestilence, War and Earthquake, never light
Upon its mountain-peaks; blind vultures, they
Sail onward far upon their fatal way:
The wingèd storms, chanting their thunder-psalm
To other lands, leave azure chasms of calm
Over this isle, or weep themselves in dew,
From which its fields and woods ever renew
Their green and golden immortality.
And from the sea there rise, and from the sky
There fall, clear exhalations, soft and bright,
Veil after veil, each hiding some delight,
Which Sun or Moon or zephyr draw aside,
Till the isle's beauty, like a naked bride
Glowing at once with love and loveliness,
Blushes and trembles at its own excess:
Yet, like a buried lamp, a Soul no less
Burns in the heart of this delicious isle,

[440–478]

An atom of th' Eternal, whose own smile
Unfolds itself, and may be felt, not seen
O'er the gray rocks, blue waves, and forests green,
Filling their bare and void interstices. –
But the chief marvel of the wilderness
Is a lone dwelling, built by whom or how
None of the rustic island-people know:
'Tis not a tower of strength, though with its height
It overtops the woods; but, for delight,
Some wise and tender Ocean-King, ere crime
Had been invented, in the world's young prime,
Reared it, a wonder of that simple time,
An envy of the isles, a pleasure-house
Made sacred to his sister and his spouse.
It scarce seems now a wreck of human art,
But, as it were Titanic; in the heart
Of Earth having assumed its form, then grown
Out of the mountains, from the living stone,
Lifting itself in caverns light and high:
For all the antique and learnèd imagery
Has been erased, and in the place of it
The ivy and the wild-vine interknit
The volumes of their many-twining stems;
Parasite flowers illume with dewy gems
The lampless halls, and when they fade, the sky
Peeps through their winter-woof of tracery
With moonlight patches, or star atoms keen,
Or fragments of the day's intense serene; –
Working mosaic on their Parian floors.
And, day and night, aloof, from the high towers
And terraces, the Earth and Ocean seem
To sleep in one another's arms, and dream
Of waves, flowers, clouds, woods, rocks, and all that we
Read in their smiles, and call reality.

This isle and house are mine, and I have vowed
Thee to be lady of the solitude. –
And I have fitted up some chambers there
Looking towards the golden Eastern air,

[479–516]

And level with the living winds, which flow
Like waves above the living waves below. –
I have sent books and music there, and all
Those instruments with which high Spirits call
The future from its cradle, and the past
Out of its grave, and make the present last
In thoughts and joys which sleep, but cannot die,
Folded within their own eternity.
Our simple life wants little, and true taste
Hires not the pale drudge Luxury, to waste
The scene it would adorn, and therefore still,
Nature with all her children haunts the hill.
The ring-dove, in the embowering ivy, yet
Keeps up her love-lament, and the owls flit
Round the evening tower, and the young stars glance
Between the quick bats in their twilight dance;
The spotted deer bask in the fresh moonlight
Before our gate, and the slow, silent night
Is measured by the pants of their calm sleep.
Be this our home in life, and when years heap
Their withered hours, like leaves, on our decay,
Let us become the overhanging day,
The living soul of this Elysian isle,
Conscious, inseparable, one. Meanwhile
We two will rise, and sit, and walk together,
Under the roof of blue Ionian weather,
And wander in the meadows, or ascend
The mossy mountains, where the blue heavens bend
With lightest winds, to touch their paramour;
Or linger, where the pebble-paven shore,
Under the quick, faint kisses of the sea
Trembles and sparkles as with ecstasy,
Possessing and possessed by all that is
Within that calm circumference of bliss,
And by each other, till to love and live
Be one: – or, at the noontide hour, arrive
Where some old cavern hoar seems yet to keep
The moonlight of the expired night asleep,
Through which the awakened day can never peep;

A veil for our seclusion, close as night's,
Where secure sleep may kill thine innocent lights;
Sleep, the fresh dew of languid love, the rain
Whose drops quench kisses till they burn again.
And we will talk, until thought's melody
Become too sweet for utterance, and it die
In words, to live again in looks, which dart
With thrilling tone into the voiceless heart,
Harmonizing silence without a sound.
Our breath shall intermix, our bosoms bound,
And our veins beat together; and our lips
With other eloquence than words, eclipse
The soul that burns between them, and the wells
Which boil under our being's inmost cells,
The fountains of our deepest life, shall be
Confused in Passion's golden purity,
As mountain-springs under the morning sun.
We shall become the same, we shall be one
Spirit within two frames, oh! wherefore two?
One passion in twin-hearts, which grows and grew,
Till like two meteors of expanding flame,
Those spheres instinct with it become the same,
Touch, mingle, are transfigured; ever still
Burning, yet ever inconsumable:
In one another's substance finding food,
Like flames too pure and light and unimbued
To nourish their bright lives with baser prey,
Which point to Heaven and cannot pass away:
One hope within two wills, one will beneath
Two overshadowing minds, one life, one death,
One Heaven, one Hell, one immortality,
And one annihilation. Woe is me!
The wingèd words on which my soul would pierce
Into the height of Love's rare Universe,
Are chains of lead around its flight of fire –
I pant, I sink, I tremble, I expire! . . .

Love's last retreat

. . . My greatest content would be utterly to desert all human society. I would retire with you & our child to a solitary island in the sea, would build a boat, & shut upon my retreat the floodgates of the world. – I would read no reviews & talk with no authors. – If I dared trust my imagination it would tell me that there were two or three chosen companions beside yourself whom I should desire. – But to this I would not listen. – Where two or three are gathered together the devil is among them, and good far more than evil impulses – love far more than hatred – has been to me, except as you have been its object, the source of all sort[s] of mischief. So on this plan I would be *alone* & would devote either to oblivion or to future generations the overflowings of a mind which, timely withdrawn from the contagion, should be kept fit for no baser object – But this it does not appear that we shall do. –

The other side of the alternative (for a medium ought not to be adopted) – is to form for ourselves a society of our own class, as much as possible, in intellect or in feelings: & to connect ourselves with the interests of that society. – Our roots were never struck so deeply as at Pisa & the transplanted tree flourishes not. – People who lead the lives which we led until last winter are like a family of Wahabee Arabs pitching their tent in the midst of London. – We must do one thing or the other: for yourself for our child, for our existence – . . .

Two comments on Epipsychidion

. . . The *Epipsychidion* is a mystery – As to real flesh & blood, you know that I do not deal in those articles, – you might as well go to a ginshop for a leg of mutton, as expect anything human or earthly from me. I desired Ollier not to circulate this piece except to the Συνετοι,* and even they it seems are inclined to approximate me to the circle of a servant girl & her sweetheart. – But I intend to write a *Symposium* of my own to set all this right.

* * *

The *Epipsychidion* I cannot look at; the person it celebrates was a cloud instead of a Juno; and poor Ixion starts from the centaur that was the offspring of his own embrace. If you are anxious, however, to hear what I am and have been, it will tell you something thereof. It is an idealized history of my life and feelings. I think one is always in love with something or other; the error, and I confess it is not easy for spirits cased in flesh and blood to avoid it, consists in seeking in a mortal image the likeness of what is perhaps eternal . . .

* Initiated [*ed.*]

A Venus Anadyomene

She seems to have just issued from the bath, and yet to be animated with the enjoyment of it. She seems all soft and mild enjoyment, and the curved lines of her fine limbs flow into each other with never-ending continuity of sweetness. Her face expresses a breathless yet passive and innocent voluptuousness without affectation, without doubt; it is at once desire and enjoyment and the pleasure arising from both. Her lips which are without the sublimity of lofty and impetuous passion like [. . .] or the grandeur of enthusiastic imagination like the Apollo of the Capitol, or an union of both like the Apollo Belvedere, have the tenderness of arch yet pure and affectionate desire, and the mode in which the ends are drawn in yet opened by the smile which forever circles round them, and the tremulous curve into which they are wrought by inextinguishable desire, and the tongue lying against the lower lip as in the listlessness of passive joy, express love, still love.

Her eyes seem heavy and swimming with pleasure, and her small forehead fades on both sides into that sweet swelling and then declension of the bone over the eye and prolongs itself to the cheek in that mode which expresses simple and tender feelings.

The neck is full and swollen as with the respiration of delight and flows with gentle curves into her perfect form.

Her form is indeed perfect. She is half sitting on and half rising from a shell, and the fulness of her limbs, and their complete roundness and perfection, do not diminish the vital energy with which they seem to be embued. The mode in which the lines of the curved back flow into and around the thighs, and the wrinkled muscles of the belly, wrinkled by the attitude, is truly astonishing. The attitude of her arms which are lovely beyond imagination is natural, unaffected, and unforced. This perhaps is the finest personification of Venus, the Deity of superficial desire, in all antique statuary. Her pointed and pear-like bosom ever virgin – the virgin Mary might have this beauty, but alas! . . .

7

Love Lyrics

To Harriet

Thy look of love has power to calm
   The stormiest passion of my soul;
Thy gentle words are drops of balm
   In life's too bitter bowl;
No grief is mine, but that alone   5
These choicest blessings I have known.

Harriet! if all who long to live
   In the warm sunshine of thine eye,
That price beyond all pain must give, —
   Beneath thy scorn to die;   10
Then hear thy chosen own too late
His heart most worthy of thy hate.

Be thou, then, one among mankind
   Whose heart is harder not for state,
Thou only virtuous, gentle, kind,   15
   Amid a world of hate;
And by a slight endurance seal
A fellow-being's lasting weal.

For pale with anguish is his cheek,
   His breath comes fast, his eyes are dim,   20
Thy name is struggling ere he speak,
   Weak is each trembling limb;
In mercy let him not endure
The misery of a fatal cure.

Oh, trust for once no erring guide!   25
   Bid the remorseless feeling flee;
'Tis malice, 'tis revenge, 'tis pride,
   'Tis anything but thee;
Oh, deign a nobler pride to prove,
And pity if thou canst not love.   30

Lines

I

The cold earth slept below,
    Above the cold sky shone;
And all around, with a chilling sound,
    From caves of ice and fields of snow,
    The breath of night like death did flow   5
    Beneath the sinking moon.

II

The wintry hedge was black,
    The green grass was not seen,
The birds did rest on the bare thorn's breast,
    Whose roots, beside the pathway track,   10
    Had bound their folds o'er many a crack
    Which the frost had made between.

III

Thine eyes glowed in the glare
    Of the moon's dying light;
As a fen-fire's beam on a sluggish stream   15
    Gleams dimly, so the moon shone there,
    And it yellowed the strings of thy raven hair,
    That shook in the wind of night.

IV

The moon made thy lips pale, beloved—
    The wind made thy bosom chill—
The night did shed on thy dear head   21
    Its frozen dew, and thou didst lie
    Where the bitter breath of the naked sky
    Might visit thee at will.

To Constantia, Singing

I

Thus to be lost and thus to sink and die,
  Perchance were death indeed!—Constantia, turn!
In thy dark eyes a power like light doth lie,
  Even though the sounds which were thy voice, which burn
Between thy lips, are laid to sleep;   5
  Within thy breath, and on thy hair, like odour, it is yet,
And from thy touch like fire doth leap.
  Even while I write, my burning cheeks are wet,
  Alas, that the torn heart can bleed, but not forget!

II

A breathless awe, like the swift change   10
  Unseen, but felt in youthful slumbers,
Wild, sweet, but incommunicably strange,
  Thou breathest now in fast ascending numbers.
The cope of heaven seems rent and cloven
  By the enchantment of thy strain,   15
And on my shoulders wings are woven,
  To follow its sublime career
Beyond the mighty moons that wane
  Upon the verge of Nature's utmost sphere,
  Till the world's shadowy walls are past and disappear. 20

III

Her voice is hovering o'er my soul—it lingers
  O'ershadowing it with soft and lulling wings,
The blood and life within those snowy fingers
  Teach witchcraft to the instrumental strings.
My brain is wild, my breath comes quick—   25
  The blood is listening in my frame,
And thronging shadows, fast and thick,
  Fall on my overflowing eyes;
My heart is quivering like a flame;
  As morning dew, that in the sunbeam dies,   30
  I am dissolved in these consuming ecstasies.

IV

I have no life, Constantia, now, but thee,
　　Whilst, like the world-surrounding air, thy song
Flows on, and fills all things with melody. —
　　Now is thy voice a tempest swift and strong,　　　　35
On which, like one in trance upborne,
　　Secure o'er rocks and waves I sweep,
Rejoicing like a cloud of morn.
　　Now 'tis the breath of summer night,
Which when the starry waters sleep,　　　　　　　　40
　　Round western isles, with incense-blossoms bright,
　　Lingering, suspends my soul in its voluptuous flight.

On Fanny Godwin

Her voice did quiver as we parted,
　　Yet knew I not that heart was broken
From which it came, and I departed
　　Heeding not the words then spoken.
　　　　Misery—O Misery,　　　　　　　　　　5
　　　　This world is all too wide for thee.

Fragment: *Amor Aeternus*

Wealth and dominion fade into the mass
  Of the great sea of human right and wrong,
When once from our possession they must pass;
  But love, though misdirected, is among
The things which are immortal, and surpass   5
  All that frail stuff which will be—or which was.

Fragment: *Igniculus Desiderii*
(Phantom of Desire)

To thirst and find no fill—to wail and wander
With short unsteady steps—to pause and ponder—
To feel the blood run through the veins and tingle
Where busy thought and blind sensation mingle;
To nurse the image of unfelt caresses   5
Till dim imagination just possesses
The half-created shadow, then all the night
Sick . . .

Song for 'Tasso'

I

I loved—alas! our life is love;
But when we cease to breathe and move
I do suppose love ceases too.
I thought, but not as now I do,
Keen thoughts and bright of linkèd lore,   5
Of all that men had thought before,
And all that Nature shows, and more.

II

And still I love and still I think,
But strangely, for my heart can drink
The dregs of such despair, and live,   10
And love; . . .
And if I think, my thoughts come fast,
I mix the present with the past,
And each seems uglier than the last.

III

Sometimes I see before me flee   15
A silver spirit's form, like thee,
O Leonora, and I sit
. . . still watching it,
Till by the grated casement's ledge
It fades, with such a sigh, as sedge   20
Breathes o'er the breezy streamlet's edge.

Asia's Song from *Prometheus Unbound*

My soul is an enchanted boat,
　Which, like a sleeping swan, doth float
Upon the silver waves of thy sweet singing;
　And thine doth like an angel sit
　Beside the helm conducting it,   5
Whilst all the winds with melody are ringing.
　It seems to float ever, for ever,
　Upon that many-winding river,
　Between mountains, woods, abysses,
　A paradise of wildernesses!   10
Till, like one in slumber bound,
Borne to the ocean, I float down, around,
Into a sea profound, of ever-spreading sound:

　Meanwhile thy spirit lifts its pinions
　In music's most serene dominions;   15
Catching the winds that fan that happy heaven.
　And we sail on, away, afar,
　Without a course, without a star,
But, by the instinct of sweet music driven;
　Till through Elysian garden islets   20
　By thee, most beautiful of pilots,
　Where never mortal pinnace glided,
　The boat of my desire is guided:
Realms where the air we breathe is love,
Which in the winds and on the waves doth move,   25
Harmonizing this earth with what we feel above.

We have passed Age's icy caves.
And Manhood's dark and tossing waves,
And Youth's smooth ocean, smiling to betray:
   Beyond the glassy gulfs we flee   30
   Of shadow-peopled Infancy,
Through Death and Birth, to a diviner day;
   A paradise of vaulted bowers,
   Lit by downward-gazing flowers,
   And watery paths that wind between   35
   Wildernesses calm and green,
Peopled by shapes too bright to see,
And rest, having beheld; somewhat like thee;
Which walk upon the sea, and chant melodiously!

An Exhortation

Chameleons feed on light and air:
   Poets' food is love and fame:
If in this wide world of care
   Poets could but find the same
With as little toil as they,   5
    Would they ever change their hue
    As the light chameleons do,
Suiting it to every ray
     Twenty times a day?

Poets are on this cold earth,   10
    As chameleons might be,
Hidden from their early birth
    In a cave beneath the sea;
Where light is, chameleons change:
    Where love is not, poets do: 15
    Fame is love disguised: if few
Find either, never think it strange
     That poets range.

Yet dare not stain with wealth or power
    A poet's free and heavenly mind: 20
If bright chameleons should devour
    Any food but beams and wind,
They would grow as earthly soon
    As their brother lizards are.
    Children of a sunnier star,   25
Spirits from beyond the moon,
     Oh, refuse the boon!

The Indian Serenade

I

I arise from dreams of thee
In the first sweet sleep of night.
When the winds are breathing low,
And the stars are shining bright:
I arise from dreams of thee,   5
And a spirit in my feet
Hath led me – who knows how?
To thy chamber window, Sweet!

II

The wandering airs they faint
On the dark, the silent stream—   10
The Champak odours fail
Like sweet thoughts in a dream;
The nightingale's complaint,
It dies upon her heart;—
As I must on thine,   15
Oh, belovèd as thou art!

III

Oh lift me from the grass!
I die! I faint! I fail!
Let thy love in kisses rain
On my lips and eyelids pale.   20
My cheek is cold and white, alas!
My heart beats loud and fast;—
Oh! press it to thine own again,
Where it will break at last.

To Sophia [Miss Stacey]

I

Thou art fair, and few are fairer
  Of the Nymphs of earth or ocean;
They are robes that fit the wearer –
  Those soft limbs of thine, whose motion
Ever falls and shifts and glances
As the life within them dances.

II

Thy deep eyes, a double Planet,
  Gaze the wisest into madness
With soft clear fire,—the winds that fan it
  Are those thoughts of tender gladness
Which, like zephyrs on the billow,
Make thy gentle soul their pillow.

III

If, whatever face thou paintest
  In those eyes, grows pale with pleasure,
If the fainting soul is faintest,   15
  When it hears thy harp's wild measure,
Wonder not that when thou speakest
Of the weak my heart is weakest.

IV

As dew beneath the wind of morning,
  As the sea which whirlwinds waken,   20
As the birds at thunder's warning,
  As aught mute yet deeply shaken,
As one who feels an unseen spirit
Is my heart when thine is near it.

To William Shelley

(With what truth may I say –
Roma! Roma! Roma!
Non è più come era prima!)

I

My lost William, thou in whom
  Some bright spirit lived, and did
That decaying robe consume
  Which its lustre faintly hid, —
Here its ashes find a tomb,   5
  But beneath this pyramid
Thou art not – if a thing divine
Like thee can die, thy funeral shrine
Is thy mother's grief and mine.

II

Where art thou, my gentle child?   10
  Let me think thy spirit feeds,
With its life intense and mild,
  The love of living leaves and weeds
Among these tombs and ruins wild; —
  Let me think that through low seeds   15
Of sweet flowers and sunny grass
Into their hues and scents may pass
A portion——

To Mary Shelley

My dearest Mary, wherefore hast thou gone,
And left me in this dreary world alone?
Thy form is here indeed—a lovely one—
But thou art fled, gone down the dreary road,
That leads to Sorrow's most obscure abode;   5
Thou sittest on the hearth of pale despair,
                                    Where
For thine own sake I cannot follow thee.

Love's Philosophy

I

The fountains mingle with the river
  And the rivers with the Ocean,
The winds of Heaven mix for ever
  With a sweet emotion;
Nothing in the world is single;   5
  All things by a law divine
In one spirit meet and mingle.
  Why not I with thine?—

II

See the mountains kiss high Heaven
  And the waves clasp one another;   10
No sister-flower would be forgiven
  If it disdained its brother;
And the sunlight clasps the earth
  And the moonbeams kiss the sea:
What is all this sweet work worth   15
  If thou kiss not me?

The Birth of Pleasure

At the creation of the Earth
Pleasure, that divinest birth,
From the soil of Heaven did rise,
Wrapped in sweet wild melodies—
Like an exhalation wreathing   5
To the sound of air low-breathing
Through Aeolian pines, which make
A shade and shelter to the lake
Whence it rises soft and slow;
Her life-breathing [limbs] did flow   10
In the harmony divine
Of an ever-lengthening line
Which enwrapped her perfect form
With a beauty clear and warm.

Fragment: Wedded Souls

I am as a spirit who has dwelt
Within his heart of hearts, and I have felt
His feelings, and have thought his thoughts, and known
The inmost converse of his soul, the tone
Unheard but in the silence of his blood,   5
When all the pulses in their multitude
Image the trembling calm of summer seas.
I have unlocked the golden melodies
Of his deep soul, as with a master-key,
And loosened them and bathed myself therein—   10
Even as an eagle in a thunder-mist
Clothing his wings with lightning.

Fragment: 'Is it
that in some Brighter Sphere'

Is it that in some brighter sphere
We part from friends we meet with here?
Or do we see the Future pass
Over the Present's dusky glass?
Or what is that that makes us seem   5
To patch up fragments of a dream,
Part of which comes true, and part
Beats and trembles in the heart?

Fragment: 'Wake the Serpent Not'

Wake the serpent not—lest he
Should not know the way to go, —
Let him crawl which yet lies sleeping
Through the deep grass of the meadow!
Not a bee shall hear him creeping,   5
Not a may-fly shall awaken
From its cradling blue-bell shaken,
Not the starlight as he's sliding
Through the grass with silent gliding.

The Two Spirits: An Allegory

First Spirit.
O Thou, who plumed with strong desire
   Wouldst float above the earth, beware!
A Shadow tracks they flight of fire—
      Night is coming!
   Bright are the regions of the air,   5
And among the winds and beams
   It were delight to wander there—
      Night is coming!

Second Spirit.
The deathless stars are bright above;
   If I would cross the shade of night,   10
Within my heart is the lamp of love,
      And that is day!
   And the moon will smile with gentle light
On my golden plumes where'er they move;
   The meteors will linger round my flight,   15
      And make night day.

First Spirit.
But if the whirlwinds of darkness waken
   Hail, and lightning, and stormy rain;
See, the bounds of the air are shaken—
      Night is coming!   20
   The red swift clouds of the hurricane
Yon declining sun have overtaken,
   The clash of the hail sweeps over the plain—
      Night is coming!

Second Spirit.

I see the light, and I hear the sound;   25
 I'll sail on the flood of the tempest dark,
With the calm within and the light around
  Which makes night day:
 And thou, when the gloom is deep and stark,
Look from thy dull earth, slumber-bound,   30
 My moon-like flight thou then mayst mark
  On high, far away.

To the Moon

 Art thou pale for weariness
Of climbing heaven and gazing on the earth,
 Wandering companionless
Among the stars that have a different birth, —
And ever changing, like a joyless eye   5
That finds no object worth its constancy?

The World's Wanderers

I

Tell me, thou Star, whose wings of light
Speed thee in thy fiery flight,
In what cavern of the night
      Will thy pinions close now?

II

Tell me, Moon, thou pale and gray
Pilgrim of Heaven's homeless way,
In what depth of night or day
      Seekest thou repose now?

III

Weary Wind, who wanderest
Like the world's rejected guest,
Hast thou still some secret nest
      On the tree or billow?

Good-Night

I

Good-night? ah! no; the hour is ill
  Which severs those it should unite;
Let us remain together still,
  Then it will be *good* night.

II

How can I call the lone night good,   5
  Though thy sweet wishes wing its flight?
Be it not said, thought, understood—
  Then it will be—*good* night.

III

To hearts which near each other move
  From evening close to morning light,   10
The night is good; because, my love,
  They never *say* good-night.

To Night

I

Swiftly walk o'er the western wave,
    Spirit of Night!
Out of the misty eastern cave,
Where, all the long and lone daylight,
Thou wovest dreams of joy and fear,
Which make thee terrible and dear, —
    Swift be thy flight!

II

Wrap thy form in a mantle gray,
    Star-inwrought!
Blind with thine hair the eyes of Day;   10
Kiss her until she be wearied out,
Then wander o'er city, and sea, and land,
Touching all with thine opiate wand—
    Come, long-sought!

III

When I arose and saw the dawn,   15
    I sighed for thee;
When light rode high, and the dew was gone,
And noon lay heavy on flower and tree,
And the weary Day turned to his rest,
Lingering like an unloved guest,
    I sighed for thee.

IV

Thy brother Death came, and cried,
    Wouldst thou me?
Thy sweet child Sleep, the filmy-eyed,
Murmured like a noontide bee,   25
Shall I nestle near thy side?
Wouldst thou me?—And I replied,
    No, not thee!

v

Death will come when thou art dead,
     Soon, too soon—   30
Sleep will come when thou art fled;
Of neither would I ask the boon
I ask of thee, belovèd Night—
Swift be thine approaching flight,
     Come soon, soon!   35

To Emilia Viviani

Madonna, wherefore hast thou sent to me
  Sweet-basil and mignonette?
Embleming love and health, which never yet
In the same wreath might be.
  Alas, and they are wet!   5
Is it with thy kisses or thy tears?
  For never rain or dew
  Such fragrance drew
From plant or flower—the very doubt endears
  My sadness ever new,   10
The sighs I breathe, the tears I shed for thee.

To—

Music, when soft voices die,
Vibrates in the memory—
Odours, when sweet violets sicken,
Live within the sense they quicken.

Rose leaves, when the rose is dead,   5
Are heaped for the belovèd's bed;
And so thy thoughts, when thou art gone,
Love itself shall slumber on.

Song

I

Rarely, rarely, comest thou,
  Spirit of Delight!
Wherefore hast thou left me now
  Many a day and night?
Many a weary night and day   5
'Tis since thou art fled away.

II

How shall ever one like me
  Win thee back again?
With the joyous and the free
  Thou wilt scoff at pain.   10
Spirit false! thou hast forgot
  All but those who need thee not.

III

As a lizard with the shade
  Of a trembling leaf,
Thou with sorrow art dismayed;   15
  Even the sighs of grief
Reproach thee, that thou art not near,
And reproach thou wilt not hear.

IV

Let me set my mournful ditty
  To a merry measure;   20
Thou wilt never come for pity,
  Thou wilt come for pleasure;
Pity then will cut away
Those cruel wings, and thou wilt stay.

V

I love all that thou lovest,   25
   Spirit of Delight!
The fresh Earth in new leaves dressed,
   And the starry night;
Autumn evening, and the morn
When the golden mists are born.   30

VI

I love snow, and all the forms
   Of the radiant frost;
I love waves, and winds, and storms,
   Everything almost
Which is Nature's and may be   35
Untainted by man's misery.

VII

I love tranquil solitude,
   And such society
As is quiet, wise, and good;
   Between thee and me   40
What difference? but thou dost possess
The things I seek, not love them less.

VIII

I love Love—though he has wings,
   And like light can flee,
But above all other things,   45
   Spirit, I love thee—
Thou art love and life! Oh, come,
Make once more my heart thy home.

The Aziola

I

'Do you not hear the Aziola cry?
    Me thinks she must be nigh,'
      Said Mary, as we sate
In dusk, ere stars were lit, or candles brought;
      And I, who thought   5
  This Aziola was some tedious woman,
    Asked, 'Who is Aziola?' How elate
I felt to know that it was nothing human,
    No mockery of myself to fear or hate;
      And Mary saw my soul,   10
And laughed, and said, 'Disquiet yourself not;
    'Tis nothing but a little downy owl.'

II

Sad Aziola! many an eventide
    Thy music I had heard
By wood and stream, meadow and mountain-side, 15
    And fields and marshes wide, —
Such as nor voice, nor lute, nor wind, nor bird,
    The soul ever stirred;
Unlike and far sweeter than them all.
Sad Aziola! from that moment I   20
    Loved thee and thy sad cry.

To Edward Williams

I

The serpent is shut out from Paradise.
    The wounded deer must seek the herb no more
      In which its heart-cure lies:
    The widowed dove must cease to haunt a bower
Like that from which its mate with feignèd sighs   5
      Fled in the April hour.
    I too must seldom seek again
Near happy friends a mitigated pain.

II

Of hatred I am proud,—with scorn content;
    Indifference, that once hurt me, now is grown   10
      Itself indifferent;
    But, not to speak of love, pity alone
Can break a spirit already more than bent.
      The miserable one
    Turns the mind's poison into food,—   15
Its medicine is tears,—its evil good.

III

Therefore, if now I see you seldomer,
    Dear friends, dear *friend*! know that I only fly
      Your looks, because they stir
    Griefs that should sleep, and hopes that cannot die: 20
The very comfort that they minister
      I scarce can bear, yet I,
    So deeply is the arrow gone,
Should quickly perish if it were withdrawn.

IV

When I return to my cold home, you ask   25
    Why I am not as I have ever been.
       You spoil me for the task
    Of acting a forced part in life's dull scene,—
Of wearing on my brow the idle mask
       Of author, great or mean,   30
    In the world's carnival. I sought
Peace thus, and but in you I found it not.

V

Full half an hour, to-day, I tried my lot
    With various flowers, and every one still said,
       'She loves me—loves me not.'
    And if this meant a vision long since fled—
If it meant fortune, fame, or peace of thought—
       If it meant,—but I dread
    To speak what you may know too well:
Still there was truth in the sad oracle.   40

VI

The crane o'er seas and forests seeks her home;
    No bird so wild but has its quiet nest,
       When it no more would roam;
    The sleepless billows on the ocean's breast
Break like a bursting heart, and die in foam,   45
       And thus at length find rest:
    Doubtless there is a place of peace
Where *my* weak heart and all its throbs will cease.

VII

I asked her, yesterday, if she believed
    That I had resolution. One who *had*   50
       Would ne'er have thus relieved
    His heart with words,—but what his judgement bade
Would do, and leave the scorner unrelieved.
       These verses are too sad
    To send to you, but that I know,   55
Happy yourself, you feel another's woe.

To—

I

One word is too often profaned
    For me to profane it,
One feeling too falsely disdained
    For thee to disdain it;
One hope is too like despair   5
    For prudence to smother,
And pity from thee more dear
    Than that from another.

II

I can give not what men call love,
    But wilt thou accept not   10
The worship the heart lifts above
    And the Heavens reject not, —
The desire of the moth for the star,
    Of the night for the morrow,
The devotion to something afar   15
    From the sphere of our sorrow?

To—

I

When passion's trance is overpast,
If tenderness and truth could last,
Or live, whilst all wild feelings keep
Some mortal slumber, dark and deep,
I should not weep, I should not weep!

II

It were enough to feel, to see,
Thy soft eyes gazing tenderly,
And dream the rest—and burn and be
The secret food of fires unseen,
Couldst thou but be as thou hast been.   10

III

After the slumber of the year
The woodland violets reappear;
All things revive in field or grove,
And sky and sea, but two, which move
And form all others, life and love.   15

Fragment: 'I would not be a King'

I would not be a king—enough
  Of woe it is to love;
The path to power is steep and rough,
  And tempests reign above.
I would not climb the imperial throne;   5
'Tis built on ice which fortune's sun
  Thaws in the height of noon.
Then farewell, king, yet were I one,
  Care would not come so soon.
Would he and I were far away   10
Keeping flocks on Himalay!

Archy's Song from
'Charles the First'

Heigho! the lark and the owl!
  One flies the morning, and one lulls the night:—
Only the nightingale, poor fond soul,
  Sings like the fool through darkness and light.

'A widow bird sate mourning for her love
  Upon a wintry bough;   10
The frozen wind crept on above,
  The freezing stream below.

'There was no leaf upon the forest bare,
  No flower upon the ground,
And little motion in the air   15
  Except the mill-wheel's sound.'

The Zucca

I

Summer was dead and Autumn was expiring,
  And infant Winter laughed upon the land
All cloudlessly and cold;—when I, desiring
  More in this world than any understand,
Wept o'er the beauty, which, like sea retiring,   5
  Had left the earth bare as the wave-worn sand
Of my lorn heart, and o'er the grass and flowers
Pale for the falsehood of the flattering Hours.

II

Summer was dead, but I yet lived to weep
  The instability of all but weeping;   10
And on the Earth lulled in her winter sleep
  I woke, and envied her as she was sleeping.
Too happy Earth! over thy face shall creep
  The wakening vernal airs, until thou, leaping
From unremembered dreams, shalt [   ] see   15
No death divide thy immortality.

III

I loved—oh, no, I mean not one of ye,
  Or any earthly one, though ye are dear
As human heart to human heart may be;—
  I loved, I know not what—but this low sphere   20
And all that it contains, contains not thee,
  Thou, whom, seen nowhere, I feel everywhere.
From Heaven and Earth, and all that in them are,
Veiled art thou, like a [   ] star.

IV

By Heaven and Earth, from all whose shapes thou   25
    flowest,
    Neither to be contained, delayed, nor hidden;
Making divine the loftiest and the lowest,
    When for a moment thou art not forbidden
To live within the life which thou bestowest;
    And leaving noblest things vacant and chidden,   30
Cold as a corpse after the spirit's flight,
Blank as the sun after the birth of night.

V

In winds, and trees, and streams, and all things common,
    In music and the sweet unconscious tone
Of animals, and voices which are human,   35
    Meant to express some feelings of their own;
In the soft motions and rare smile of woman,
    In flowers and leaves, and in the grass fresh-shown,
Or dying in the autumn, I the most
Adore thee present or lament thee lost.   40

VI

And thus I went lamenting, when I saw
    A plant upon the river's margin lie,
Like one who loved beyond his nature's law,
    And in despair had cast him down to die;
Its leaves, which had outlived the frost, the thaw   45
    Had blighted; like a heart which hatred's eye
Can blast not, but which pity kills; the dew
Lay on its spotted leaves like tears too true.

VII

The Heavens had wept upon it, but the Earth
    Had crushed it on her unmaternal breast [   ]   50

    .   .   .   .

VIII

I bore it to my chamber, and I planted
  It in a vase full of the lightest mould;
The winter beams which out of Heaven slanted
  Fell through the window-panes, disrobed of cold,
Upon its leaves and flowers; the stars which panted   55
  In evening for the Day, whose car has rolled
Over the horizon's wave, with looks of light
Smiled on it from the threshold of the night.

IX

The mitigated influence of air
  And light revived the plant, and from it grew   60
Strong leaves and tendrils, and its flowers fair,
  Full as a cup with the vine's burning dew,
O'erflowed with golden colours; an atmosphere
  Of vital warmth enfolded it anew,
And every impulse sent to every part   65
The unbeheld pulsations of its heart.

X

Well might the plant grow beautiful and strong,
  Even if the air and sun had smiled not on it;
For one wept o'er it all the winter long
  Tears pure as Heaven's rain, which fell upon it   70
Hour after hour; for sounds of softest song
  Mixed with the stringèd melodies that won it
To leave the gentle lips on which it slept,
Had loosed the heart of him who sat and wept.

XI

Had loosed his heart, and shook the leaves and flowers   75
  On which he wept, the while the savage storm
Waked by the darkest of December's hours
  Was raving round the chamber hushed and warm;
The birds were shivering in their leafless bowers,
  The fish were frozen in the pools, the form   80
Of every summer plant was dead [   ]
Whilst this [   ]

. . . .

Lines: 'When the Lamp
is Shattered'

I

When the lamp is shattered
The light in the dust lies dead—
   When the cloud is scattered
The rainbow's glory is shed.
   When the lute is broken,   5
Sweet tones are remembered not;
   When the lips have spoken,
Loved accents are soon forgot.

II

As music and splendour
Survive not the lamp and the lute,   10
   The heart's echoes render
No song when the spirit is mute:—
   No song but sad dirges,
Like the wind through a ruined cell,
   Or the mournful surges   15
That ring the dead seaman's knell.

III

When hearts have once mingled
Love first leaves the well-built nest;
   The weak one is singled
To endure what it once possessed.   20
   O Love! who bewailest
The frailty of all things here,
   Why choose you the frailest
For your cradle, your home, and your bier?

IV

Its passions will rock thee   25
As the storms rock the ravens on high;
  Bright reason will mock thee,
Like the sun from a wintry sky.
  From thy nest every rafter
Will rot, and thine eagle home   30
  Leave thee naked to laughter,
When leaves fall and cold winds come.

With a Guitar, To Jane

Ariel to Miranda:—Take
This slave of Music, for the sake
Of him who is the slave of thee,
And teach it all the harmony
In which thou canst, and only thou,   5
Make the delighted spirit glow,
Till joy denies itself again,
And, too intense, is turned to pain;
For by permission and command
Of thine own Prince Ferdinand,   10
Poor Ariel sends this silent token
Of more than ever can be spoken;
Your guardian spirit, Ariel, who,
From life to life, must still pursue
Your happiness;—for thus alone   15
Can Ariel ever find his own.
From Prospero's enchanted cell,
As the mighty verses tell,
To the throne of Naples, he
Lit you o'er the trackless sea,   20
Flitting on, your prow before,
Like a living meteor.
When you die, the silent Moon,
In her interlunar swoon,
Is not sadder in her cell   25
Than deserted Ariel.
When you live again on earth,
Like an unseen star of birth,
Ariel guides you o'er the sea
Of life from your nativity.   30
Many changes have been run
Since Ferdinand and you begun
Your course of love, and Ariel still
Has tracked your steps, and served
    your will;

Now, in humbler, happier lot,   35
This is all remembered not;
And now, alas! the poor sprite is
Imprisoned, for some fault of his,
In a body like a grave;—
From you he only dares to crave,   40
For his service and his sorrow,
A smile to-day, a song to-morrow.
The artist who this idol wrought,
To echo all harmonious thought,
Felled a tree, while on the steep   45
The woods were in their winter sleep,
Rocked in that repose divine
On the wind-swept Apennine;
And dreaming, some of Autumn past,
And some of Spring approaching
    fast,   50
And some of April buds and showers,
And some of songs in July bowers,
And all of love; and so this tree,—
O that such our death may be!—
Died in sleep, and felt no pain,   55
To live in happier form again:
From which, beneath Heaven's fairest
    star,
The artist wrought this loved Guitar,
And taught it justly to reply,
To all who question skilfully,   60
In language gentle as thine own;
Whispering in enamoured tone
Sweet oracles of woods and dells,
And summer winds in sylvan cells;
For it had learned all harmonies   65
Of the plains and of the skies,
Of the forests and the mountains,
And the many-voicèd fountains;
The clearest echoes of the hills,
The softest notes of falling rills,   70
The melodies of birds and bees,

The murmuring of summer seas,
And pattering rain, and breathing
    dew,
And airs of evening; and it knew   75
That seldom-heard mysterious sound,
Which, driven on its diurnal round,
As it floats through boundless day,
Our world enkindles on its way.—
All this it knows, but will not tell
To those who cannot question well   80
The Spirit that inhabits it;
It talks according to the wit
Of its companions; and no more
Is heard than has been felt before,
By those who tempt it to betray   85
These secrets of an elder day:
But, sweetly as its answers will
Flatter hands of perfect skill,
It keeps its highest, holiest tone
For our belovèd Jane alone.   90

Lines Written in the Bay of Lerici

She left me at the silent time
When the moon had ceased to climb
The azure path of Heaven's steep,
And like an albatross asleep,
Balanced on her wings of light,   5
Hovered in the purple night,
Ere she sought her ocean nest
In the chambers of the West.
She left me, and I stayed alone
Thinking over every tone   10
Which, though silent to the ear,
The enchanted heart could hear,
Like notes which die when born, but still
Haunt the echoes of the hill;
And feeling ever—oh, too much!—   15
The soft vibration of her touch,
As if her gentle hand, even now,
Lightly trembled on my brow;
And thus, although she absent were,
Memory gave me all of her   20
That even Fancy dares to claim:—
Her presence had made weak and tame
All passions, and I lived alone
In the time which is our own;
The past and future were forgot,   25
As they had been, and would be, not.
But soon, the guardian angel gone,
The daemon reassumed his throne
In my faint heart. I dare not speak
My thoughts, but thus disturbed and weak   30
I sat and saw the vessels glide
Over the ocean bright and wide,

Like spirit-wingèd chariots sent
O'er some serenest element
For ministrations strange and far;   35
As if to some Elysian star
Sailed for drink to medicine
Such sweet and bitter pain as mine.
And the wind that winged their flight
From the land came fresh and light,   40
And the scent of wingèd flowers,
And the coolness of the hours
Of dew, and sweet warmth left by day,
Were scattered o'er the twinkling bay.
And the fisher with his lamp   45
And spear about the low rocks damp
Crept, and struck the fish which came
To worship the delusive flame.
Too happy they, whose pleasure sought
Extinguishes all sense and thought   50
Of the regret that pleasure leaves,
Destroying life alone, not peace!

Fragment: To the Moon

Bright wanderer, fair coquette of Heaven,
To whom alone it has been given
To change and be adored for ever,
Envy not this dim world, for never
But once within its shadow grew
One fair as ——

Postscript

Shelley on Love

. . . He never mentioned Love but he shed a grace borrowed from his own nature, that scarcely any other poet has bestowed, on that passion. When he spoke of it as the law of life, which inasmuch as we rebel against we err and injure ourselves and others, he promulgated that which he considered an irrefragable truth. In his eyes it was the essence of our being, and all woe and pain arose from the war made against it by selfishness, or insensibility, or mistake. By reverting in his mind to this first principle, he discovered the source of many emotions, and could disclose the secrets of all hearts; and his delineations of passion and emotion touch the finest chords of our nature . . .

MARY SHELLEY, 1839

A Note on the Text

Sources for the extracts in this anthology are given below. Each title is followed by the known or likely date of *composition*. There is still no complete or perfectly reliable edition of Shelley's collected prose, so to help the general reader I have listed several major editions in which each extract may be found, usually with very slight textual differences or editorial emendations. In general I have preferred the most modern and least emended texts. I have silently modernized the spelling, and allowed square editorial brackets – [thus] – to indicate doubtful or inconsistent or missing words. However, for Shelley's poetry and letters, I have gratefully accepted the textual authority of the currently established Oxford editions.

Special acknowledgements and thanks are due to the Oxford University Press; to the editorial work of A. H. Koszul, J. A. Notopoulos, and D. L. Clark; and to Peter Jay for his examination of Shelley's Greek quotations.

Abbreviations used are as follows:

Mary Shelley, 1840	*Essays, Letters from Abroad, Translations and Fragments, by Percy Bysshe Shelley* edited by Mary Shelley. Two volumes, 1840.
Forman, 1880	*The Prose Works of Percy Bysshe Shelley* edited by H. B. Forman. Four volumes, 1880.
Koszul, 1910	*Shelley's Prose in the Bodleian Manuscripts* edited by A. H. Koszul, 1910.
Clark, 1966	*Shelley's Prose, or The Trumpet of a*

Prophecy edited by David Lee Clark. University of New Mexico Press, 1966. Reprinted, Fourth Estate, 1988.

Notopoulos, 1949   *The Platonism of Shelley* with texts edited by J. A. Notopoulos. Duke University Press, 1949.

Letters   *The Letters of Percy Bysshe Shelley* edited by F. L. Jones. Oxford University Press. Two volumes, 1964.

Poetical Works   *Shelley: Poetical Works* edited by Thomas Hutchinson. Oxford University Press, 1968.

Sources

Childhood

1 'Fragment of an Essay on Friendship', c. 1822. Texts: Forman, 1880, vol. 2. Clark, 1966.
2 *from* 'Bacchus and Ampelus' in 'Notes on Sculptures in Rome and Florence', 1819–20. Texts: Forman, 1880, vol. 3. Clark, 1966.
3 'The Laocoön' in 'Notes on Sculptures in Rome and Florence', 1819–20. Texts: Forman, 1880, vol. 3. Clark, 1966.
4 *from* 'Niobe' in 'Notes on Sculptures in Rome and Florence', 1819–20. Texts: Mary Shelley, 1840, vol. 2. Forman, 1880, vol. 3. Clark, 1966.
5 *from* 'Essay on Life', 1812–15. Texts: Mary Shelley, 1840, vol. 1. Forman, 1880, vol. 2. Clark, 1966.
6 *from* 'Catalogue of the Phenomena of Dreams', 1815. Texts: Mary Shelley, 1840, vol. 1. Forman, 1880, vol. 2. Clark, 1966.

First Love

1 Ninth Note to *Queen Mab*, c. 1812. Text: Poetical Works.
2 Letter 201, to Sir James Lawrence, 17 August 1812. Text: Letters, vol. 1.
3 *from* Chapter 1 of *The Assassins: A Romance*, 1814. Texts: Mary Shelley, 1840, vol. 1. Forman, 1880, vol. 2. Clark, 1966.
4 Letter 265, to T. J. Hogg, 3 October 1814. Text: Letters, vol. 1.

Second Marriage

1 'Essay on Love', c. 1815. Texts: Mary Shelley, 1840, vol. 1. Forman, 1880, vol. 2. Clark, 1966.
2 Preface to *Alastor, or The Spirit of Solitude*, 1815–16. Text: Poetical Works.

3 *from: Alastor, or The Spirit of Solitude*, 1815–16. Lines 75–211. Text: Poetical Works.
4 *from* 'A Fragment on Marriage', c. 1815. Texts: Koszul, 1910. Clark, 1966.
5 *from* 'A Review of T. J. Hogg's *Prince Alexy Haimatoff*', 1814. Text: Clark, 1966.
6 *from* 'Essay on Christianity', 1816–17. Text: Forman, 1880, vol. 2. Koszul, 1910. Clark, 1966.

Platonic Harmonies

1 'A Discourse on the Manners of the Ancient Greeks Relative to the Subject of Love', 1818. Texts: Mary Shelley, 1840, vol. 1 (censored version). Forman, 1880, vol. 3 (censored version). Notopoulos, 1949. Clark, 1966.
2 'Preface to the Banquet of Plato', 1818. Texts: Mary Shelley, 1840, vol. 1. Forman, 1880, vol. 3. Notopoulos, 1949. Clark, 1966.
3 'The Symposium, or The Banquet, translated from Plato', 1818. Texts: Mary Shelley, 1840, vol. 1. Forman, 1880, vol. 3. *Five Dialogues of Plato*, Everyman's Library No. 456, 1910. Notopoulos, 1949.

Italian Discords

1 *from: Julian and Maddalo*, 1818–19. Lines 141–583. Text: Poetical Works.
2 Letter 605, to Mary Shelley, 7 August 1821. Text: Letters, vol. 2.

Eternal Image

1 *from: A Defence of Poetry*, 1821. Texts: Mary Shelley, 1840, vol. 1. Forman, 1880, vol. 3. Koszul, 1910. Clark, 1966.
2 Four Prefaces to *Epipsychidion*, 1821. Text: Poetical Works.
3 *from: Epipsychidion*, 1821. Lines 72–591. Text: Poetical Works.
4 *from* Letter 656, to Mary Shelley, 15 August 1821. Text: Letters, vol. 2.
5 *from* Letter 668, to John Gisborne, 22 October 1821. Text: Letters, vol. 2.

from Letter 715, to John Gisborne, 18 June 1822. Text: *Letters,*
vol. 2.

6   'A Venus Anadyomene' in 'Notes on Sculptures in Rome and
Florence', 1819–20. Texts: Mary Shelley, 1840, vol. 2. Forman,
1880, vol. 3. Clark, 1966.

7   *from* Mary Shelley's 'Note to Rosalind and Helen', 1839. Text:
Poetical Works.

Love Lyrics

from: Shelley: Poetical Works edited by Thomas Hutchinson.
Oxford University Press, 1968.

Chronology of Shelley's Life

1792   Born in Sussex. His father a landowner and Whig MP
        aged 40; his mother a county girl and keen rider aged 29.
        Later three younger sisters and a brother.
1804   Sent to Eton.
1806   His grandfather created a Baronet by the Prince Regent.
1808   Adolescent affair with his cousin, Harriet Grove.
1810   *Zastrozzi*, a gothic love-and-horror novel, published.
        Entered University College, Oxford, following
        father's footsteps.
1811   Sent down from Oxford, with T. J. Hogg, for
        publishing and refusing to admit to authorship of *The
        Necessity of Atheism*, a pamphlet.
        Eloped with Harriet Westbrook, a 16-year-old daughter
        of a prosperous Jewish coffee-house proprietor. Married
        in Edinburgh.
        Joined by Harriet's elder sister, Eliza. Abandoned Hogg.
1812   Political activity in Ireland, Devon and North Wales.
        Met William Godwin.
        Joined by Elizabeth Hitchener, a schoolteacher from
        Sussex.
1813   First child, Ianthe, born in London.
        Poem and Notes of *Queen Mab* published, including
        essay on free love.
1814   Increasing difficulties with Harriet; lived with the
        Boinvilles.
        Met Mary Godwin in London. Repeated marriage to
        Harriet.
        Eloped with Mary, and step-sister Jane 'Claire'
        Clairmont, to France and Switzerland. Wrote *The
        Assassins*.
        Tried to arrange informal separation from Harriet; their
        second child Charles born.

1815   His grandfather died; received £1,000 annuity on entailed estate.
Shared house with Mary, Claire and Hogg.
Mary's first baby born prematurely, and dies.
Claire temporarily driven away by Mary. Wrote *Essay on Love*.

1816   *Alastor* published. Claire rejoined household. Mary's child William ('Willmouse') born.
Shelley, Mary and Claire spent the summer with Lord Byron on Lake Geneva.
Fanny Godwin (Mary's half-sister) committed suicide.
Harriet committed suicide.
Shelley married Mary.

1817   Claire's child by Byron, Allegra, born.
Ianthe and Charles removed from Shelley's custody by Chancery Court.
Shelley writing his revolutionary poem *The Revolt of Islam*, dedicated to Mary; his poem 'To Constantia' (Claire); and his *Essay on Christianity*.
Mary's third child, Clara, born. Mary published *Frankenstein*.

1818   Shelley took his entire household to Italy. Allegra sent to Byron.
Translated Plato's *Symposium*, and wrote introductory *Discourse*.
Spent time with Claire alone at Este, near Venice.
Little Clara died of teething fever; difficulties with Mary.
Wrote *Julian and Maddalo*, and began *Prometheus Unbound*.
Mysterious unhappiness at Naples; 'adopted' a baby, Elena Adelaide Shelley.

1819   Little William died at Rome; Mary suffered a nervous breakdown and wrote her autobiographical novel *Mathilda*.
Shelley continued writing *Prometheus Unbound*, and his *Notes on Sculptures*.
Mary's fourth and only surviving child, Percy, born at Florence, where Shelley wrote *Ode to the West Wind*.

1820   Shelley settled his household at Pisa; friendship with

John and Maria Gisborne.
Elena Adelaide died in Naples; Shelley blackmailed.
Wrote *The Witch of Atlas*. Claire living more
independently at Livorno, and Florence.

1821 Friendship with Emilia Viviani, a 19-year-old convent
heiress, inspired the writing of Shelley's poetic
autobiography *Epipsychidion*.
On a trip to Byron at Ravenna, Shelley heard of the
'Hoppner scandal' concerning Claire and himself at
Este and Naples.
Wrote *A Defence of Poetry, Adonais*, and *Hellas*.
Friendship with Edward and Jane Williams.

1822 Claire heard of the Hoppner scandal in Florence; she
decided to leave Italy, but was then persuaded to rejoin
the Shelleys.
Allegra died in the convent where Byron left her.
Shelley, Mary, Claire and the Williamses move to the
remote Casa Magni, on the seashore at San Terenzo near
Lerici.
Mary suffered a near-fatal miscarriage.
Shelley began his last, uncompleted poem *The Triumph
of Life* and a series of self-revealing letters to John
Gisborne in London and Horace Smith in Paris.
Shelley, Edward Williams, and Charles Vivian – the
English boatboy – drowned in their 24-foot schooner
returning to Lerici from a visit to Byron and Hunt at
Livorno.